AN INTRODUCTORY GUIDE TO

Reflexology

Louise Tucker

General Editor Jane Foulston

Published by EMS Publishing
2nd Floor Chiswick Gate,
598-608 Chiswick High Road, London, W4 5RT
0845 017 9022

First published March 2001
Reprinted November 2003
Second Edition July 2008
Revised September 2009
Reprinted October 2012
Reprinted December 2012

ISBN 978 1903348 581

Printed by Scotprint

Illustrations:
Graham Edwards
fotolia.com
istockphoto.com
sciencephoto.com

The publishers have not been able to trace the holder of the
copyright for the Iridology maps. We would be grateful for any
assistance in tracing the copyright holder.

Prepared for the publishers by Idego Media Limited.

Contents

Introduction

An Introductory Guide to Reflexology provides a concisely explained and thoroughly illustrated introduction to a complex subject. The book includes the required material for many examination syllabuses, such as ITEC and the Association of Reflexologists, and is intended for use as a textbook, as part of an accredited course, with support from a qualified tutor. It should not be considered a substitute for proper training or qualifications.

Author

Louise Tucker

Louise Tucker is a freelance writer. Previously an academic and lecturer, she has written books on various subjects, including *An Introductory Guide to Anatomy and Physiology*, also published by EMS Publishing.

General Editor

Jane Foulston

Jane Foulston has been in the beauty therapy industry for over 25 years. Jane taught beauty and complementary therapies in both further education colleges and the private sector for 14 years. She then set up a beauty therapy college in Japan before working nationally and internationally as an ITEC examiner. Since becoming its Director in 1998, ITEC has gone on to be the world's largest international awarding body for beauty therapy.

Contributing Editors

Fae Major

Fae Major has worked in the field of complementary therapy for 23 years. Her experience includes working in alternative medicine clinics and private beauty salons both in the UK and abroad. Fae also has 15 years teaching experience and became a practical examiner for ITEC in 1992. As well as continuing to examine, she is currently working for ITEC as part of the Qualifications Development team.

Marguerite Wynne

Marguerite Wynne began her career in one of London's foremost beauty salons and went on to teach in the College of Beauty Therapy in London. Subsequently she owned her own salon and school in Buckinghamshire. In 2005 Marguerite was appointed Education Manager for ITEC where she now monitors the standards and consistency of ITEC examinations.

Elaine Hall

Elaine Hall taught beauty and complementary therapies at the West of England College in Bath before managing the complementary therapies section at Bridgwater College. She ran a private salon and a clinic in a nursing home for several years and is now a senior ITEC Examiner and a member of the Qualification Development team.

Terms of reference

In order to be able to refer to the feet and their different areas without confusion throughout the book the following terms will be used for standard and easy reference:

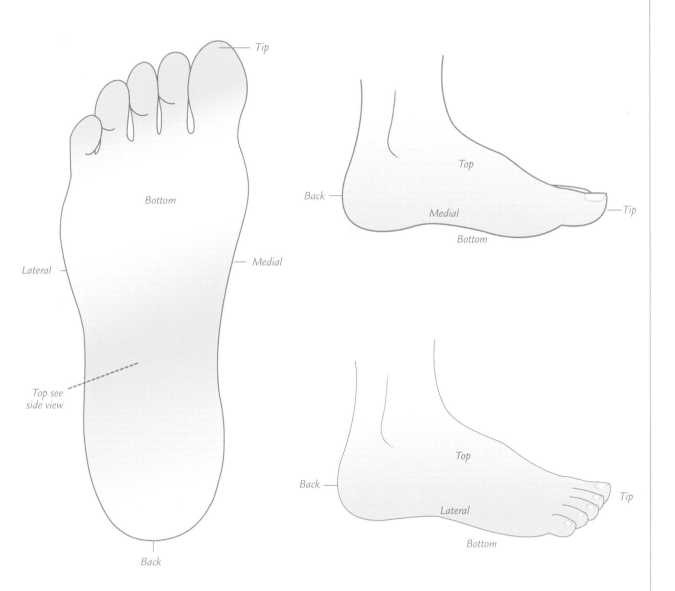

Bottom: soles of the feet, what you stand on
Top: what you see when you look down at your feet when standing
Back: heel end of foot

Tip: toe end of foot
Medial/Inside: the surface running from the big toe to the heel
Lateral/Outside: the surface running from the little toe to the heel.

Anatomical regions

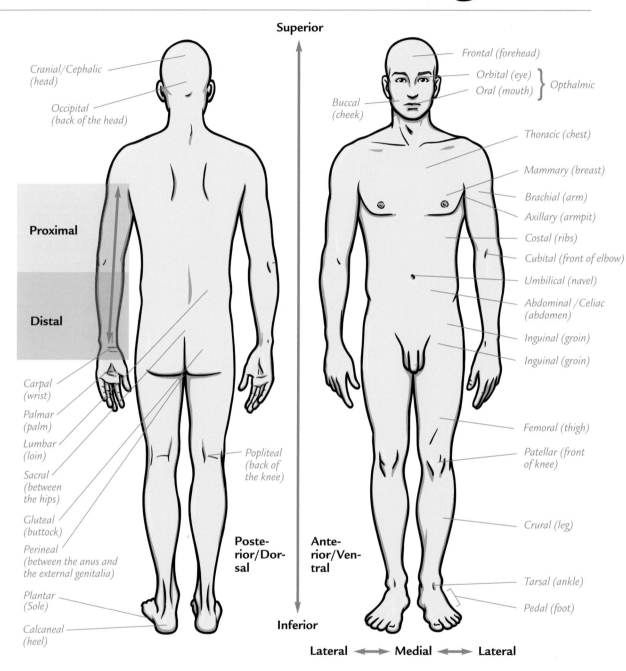

Superior

Cranial/Cephalic (head)

Occipital (back of the head)

Frontal (forehead)

Orbital (eye)
Oral (mouth)
} Opthalmic

Buccal (cheek)

Thoracic (chest)

Mammary (breast)

Brachial (arm)

Axillary (armpit)

Costal (ribs)

Cubital (front of elbow)

Umbilical (navel)

Abdominal /Celiac (abdomen)

Inguinal (groin)

Inguinal (groin)

Proximal

Distal

Carpal (wrist)

Palmar (palm)

Lumbar (loin)

Sacral (between the hips)

Gluteal (buttock)

Perineal (between the anus and the external genitalia)

Plantar (Sole)

Calcaneal (heel)

Popliteal (back of the knee)

Femoral (thigh)

Patellar (front of knee)

Crural (leg)

Tarsal (ankle)

Pedal (foot)

Poste-rior/Dor-sal

Ante-rior/Ven-tral

Inferior

Lateral ↔ Medial ↔ Lateral

Anatomical directional terms

Superficial	Towards the surface of the body
Deep	Away from the body surface
Parietal	Forming wall of body cavity
Visceral	Pertaining to an organ
Ipsilateral	On the same side of the body
Contralateral	On the opposite side of the body

Anatomical regions

Cutaneous	Skin

Body planes

Sagittal	Divides into right and left
Coronal/frontal	Divides anterior and posterior (front and back)
Transverse	Divides superior and inferior

1 History & development of reflexology

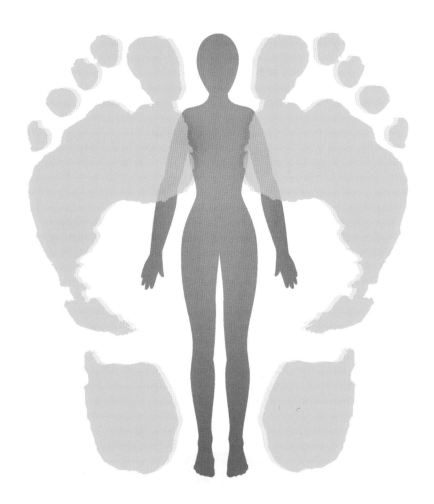

In Brief

Reflexology is a theory and therapy that uses the feet to treat the whole body. The therapy was developed by Eunice Ingham in the mid-to-late twentieth century. However, the principles behind it — massaging the feet, treating the body holistically (as a whole) and dividing the body into zones or lines of energy — date back thousands of years. This chapter provides an overview of the history and development of reflexology.

Learning objectives

The target knowledge of this chapter is:
● the history and development of reflexology.

HISTORY OF REFLEXOLOGY

The Ancients and foot massage

Massaging and touching the feet to help the body is a very ancient practice. The tomb of Ankhmahor in Egypt was found in 1897 and is thought to date back to around 2330 BC. Ankhmahor was a physician and on the wall of his tomb there are a series of pictures showing what seems to be a foot massage. One person is holding the foot of the other, appearing to massage or manipulate it. In another picture a hand massage is taking place. Feet have also always been very important to native Americans for whom massaging the feet was considered a method of maintaining physical, mental and spiritual balance.

An example of an Egyptian tomb painting depicting what appears to be a foot massage.

The Chinese

The Chinese have been using the application of pressure as a healing therapy for over 5000 years. The ancient therapy of acupressure uses thumb pressure on acupoints — a series of points along lines of energy throughout the body — to help unblock energy and thus let the body heal itself. Acupuncture is similar but needles are used instead of thumb or finger pressure. Both these therapies are thought to have influenced the development of reflexology because they are all based on the principle that there is a relationship between the point where pressure is applied and the rest of the body.

Therapy using pressure applied to parts of the body was practised in Europe from around the fourteenth century by lay practitioners and physicians. Important developments in healthcare continued in Europe during the 19th Century.

Sir Henry Head (1861-1940) was a British neurologist working in the 1890s. He conducted studies into the relationship between pressure applied to the skin and the internal organs. He demonstrated a link between the skin and the nervous system. His discoveries became known as 'Head's zones' and his studies led to the mapping of dermatomes.

Sir Charles Sherrington (1857-1952), a British neurophysiologist conducted studies into sensory dermatomes, the reflex action of the nervous system and proprioception – the ability to sense the position, location, orientation and movement of the body. In 1906 he published 'The Integrative Nervous System'. In 1932 he shared the Nobel Prize with Edgar Adrian for research into the function of neurons. He identified nociceptors, sensory nerves that initiate the sensation of pain. His studies detailed the processes and functions of nerves used to co-ordinate and control body activities. His work influenced the development of brain surgery and treatment of nervous disorders.

Alongside the developments in orthodox medicine, further work in the use of complementary therapies was continuing throughout Europe and America.

Dr William Fitzgerald and Zone Therapy

Dr William Fitzgerald, an American ear, nose and throat physician, is one of the most important people in the history of reflexology. In the early twentieth century he noticed that by pressing on one part of the body another part of the body would be anaesthetised. He experimented with different ways to apply this pressure, from pressing on the body using his fingers and thumbs to attaching pegs and clamps to the patient's fingers or asking the patient to grasp a metal comb very tightly. Eventually, he started performing minor surgery using this technique.

Using what he knew about applying pressure to one part of the body and then its effect on another part of the body, Fitzgerald divided the body into ten, longitudinal zones. These zones formed the basis for the development of reflexology and are still used today. Everything in each zone is connected so pressure on a toe at one end will affect the head at the other end. The connection between them is energy: every part of a zone is linked by energy and exists in the same energy zone. If the energy of one part is blocked, this will mean that the whole zone will also be blocked.

Did you know?

The popular wristbands used for motion sickness use a pressure, or acu-point, to relax and prevent nausea.

10

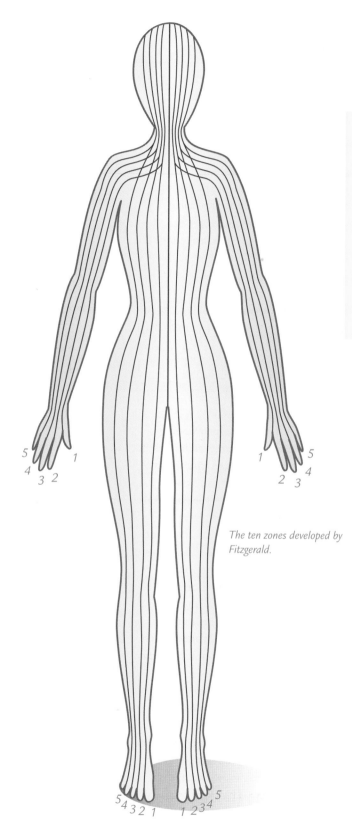

The ten zones developed by Fitzgerald.

The ten zones

It is easy to remember the ten zones: each finger or toe is part of a different one. Just as there are five fingers/toes on either side of the midline through the centre of the body there are five zones on either side of this central line. All the zones are of equal width and they run from top to bottom, front to back. Work or massage of one part of the zone will affect the whole of that zone.

The link between Zone Therapy and acupuncture

Fitzgerald worked on the basis that each zone passed through several organs and pressure at one point in the zone would cause a reflex action in another part of the zone, either stimulating muscle contraction or relaxation. Whether unconsciously or not, he had produced a system of dividing up the body's energy which resembles the meridians of energy used in acupuncture and acupressure. The most important element of this therapy is that it demonstrates the interrelationship between all the different parts of the body and this is the main principle on which reflexology is based.

From Fitzgerald to Ingham

In 1915 Dr Edwin Bowers, one of Fitzgerald's colleagues, brought Zone Therapy to the attention of the rest of the medical profession, and the public, by writing and publishing an article called 'To stop that toothache squeeze your toe'. He and Fitzgerald then published a book on the subject, *Zone Therapy*, in

1917. Most doctors were not very enthusiastic but some, like Dr Joseph Riley and his wife Elizabeth Ann Riley became interested and developed it further. The Rileys began to research the therapy and use it in their school of chiropractic in Washington DC. A physiotherapist in their school, Eunice Ingham, also became very interested in Zone Therapy and in the early 1930s, after discussions with Riley and work of her own, she developed foot reflexology.

Eunice Ingham and reflexology

Eunice Ingham developed the work of her predecessors in several ways. She became aware that if the zones ran through the whole body, some areas would be not only more accessible but also more sensitive and thus more responsive. She chose to concentrate on the feet for several reasons: she had discovered that pressure on various points on the feet helped relieve pain; she had recognised that all the nerves end in the feet and that they are not only accessible but also sensitive because, unlike the hands, they are generally kept covered up.

Since the feet were at the end of every zone, Ingham experimented to find out how pressure on one part of the foot affected other parts of the body. Having realised that the whole body could be treated using the application of pressure to the feet or hands she used Fitzgerald's zones to chart the whole body onto the feet. Her charts are now the standard used by reflexologists all over the world. Eunice Ingham spent many years lecturing on reflexology and practising it and she also wrote two books, *Stories the Feet can Tell* and *Stories the Feet have Told*, both of which remain of interest and importance to reflexology students and practitioners.

The Bayly School

Doreen Bayly brought Reflexology to Britain in 1966. She had studied with Ingham in the US and on her return she set up the Bayly School of Reflexology. In 1958, Hanne Marquardt, a German nurse, discovered the work of Eunice Ingham and began to work with her methods. Through her own practice and study over the next few years, she identified and developed the three transverse zones (shoulder, waist and pelvic) and produced comprehensive charts combining these with Fitzgerald's longitudinal zones. She described her therapy as 'Reflex zone therapy' and began training others in the techniques in the mid 1960s. In 1974 she published a book called *Reflex Zone Therapy of the Feet.*

Joseph Corvo studied the principles of Zone Therapy in America. He then went on develop his own techniques in the application of pressure to key points around the body. His methods work not only on the hands and feet, but also the face to promote good health and balance.

Reflexology in the 21st century

Reflexology has become established as one of the most popular forms of complementary therapies practised today. Research into the effects of the treatment and the techniques used continues such as the work undertaken by Lynne Booth, the originator of Vertical Reflex Therapy.

Like other complementary and holistic therapies, reflexology works on the whole person, rather than just one particular symptom. This approach, seeing the body as a whole not as separate parts is now becoming extremely common and reflexology is viewed by many as an important part of a modern, healthy lifestyle.

You now know the history of reflexology and the background to its development.

HISTORY AND DEVELOPMENT OF REFLEXOLOGY

DON'T FORGET TO LOGIN TO GAIN ACCESS TO YOUR FREE MULTI-MEDIA LEARNING RESOURCES

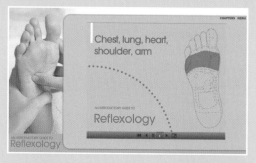

IMPROVE YOUR KNOWLEDGE WITH THE INTERACTIVE ANIMATIONS AND DIAGRAMS

TEST YOUR KNOWLEDGE WITH CROSSWORDS

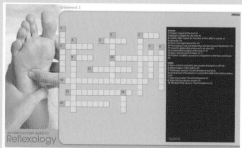

TEST YOUR KNOWLEDGE WITH FILL IN THE GAPS

AND MUCH MORE!

To login to use these resources visit www.emspublishing.co.uk/reflex and follow the onscreen instructions.

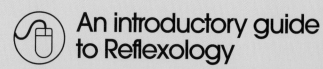

An introductory guide to Reflexology

2 Theory and concept of reflexology

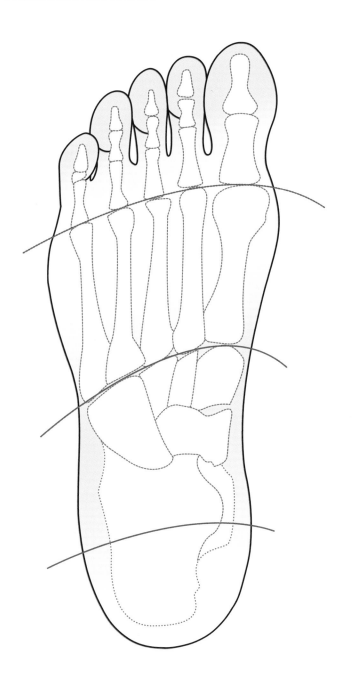

In Brief

Reflexology is a theory and therapy that uses the feet as a map, or mirror, of the whole body. By manipulating, and applying pressure to certain parts of the feet, the whole body can be 're-tuned' and brought back into balance.

Learning objectives

The target knowledge of this chapter is:

- the theory of reflexology and how it works
- the ten zones and their relation to the feet
- foot 'maps' and reflex areas
- referral areas
- the theory of hand treatments.

WHAT IS REFLEXOLOGY?

Reflexology is a therapy that treats the feet in order to balance the whole body. Its main principle is that by massaging and applying pressure to parts of the feet known as reflex areas, other corresponding and connected areas of the body will feel the benefit. In reflexology, the feet and hands are like mini-maps of the body's anatomy so any body system can be accessed and stimulated by massaging the corresponding area of the foot or hand. The aim is to stimulate the body's own healing processes in order to keep it in homeostasis, or in a homeodynamic, i.e. balanced, state. It is a holistic therapy which means that it works on the principle that the whole person must be treated: if one area of the body is out of balance then other areas will be. It encourages both relaxation and stimulation: the first helps the body rebuild its energy resources and recover from illness and disease whereas the second helps activate the circulation and the nervous system, making both more efficient and thus benefiting the body as a whole.

So it's a foot massage?

Not exactly. It uses massage techniques but, unlike massage, reflexology works with the feet as anatomical 'maps' of the whole body. By applying pressure to one part of the foot, the reflexologist aims to benefit not only the feet but also the rest of the body.

Is it a medical treatment?

No, but it helps maintain and restore health. The reflexologist can detect imbalances in the body by working on the feet and then works on problem areas accordingly to help correct them. However, it is not a cure, more a helping hand for the body's self-healing processes. Reflexology helps balance the systems of the body helping them work more efficiently which, in turn, speeds up the natural healing processes.

What are its benefits?

- it relieves stress and tension and has a deeply relaxing effect: 75% of disease is estimated to be stress-related
- in order to function, the body needs energy in the form of oxygen and nutrients which are circulated in the blood. As reflexology improves blood circulation, it thus increases the efficiency of all organs and cells
- it helps release trapped nervous energy and improves neural efficiency; approximately 7000 nerves are stimulated by reflexology massage
- it improves waste removal and elimination
- it activates the body's self-healing.

How does it work?

In order to understand the practical aspects of reflexology, it is necessary to start with the theory. Reflexology works on the principle that the whole body, from head to toe, is connected. This connection is represented by ten longitudinal zones, developed by Dr William Fitzgerald. These zones run front to back, head to toe throughout the body and are most easily accessible via the feet. By manipulating a particular area of the foot, the rest of the organs in that zone will feel a positive benefit. In a sense it is like a messaging service – when specific pressure is applied to a section of the foot, this sends a positive message along the zone. For example, working the heart area of the foot will release blocked energy, not only stimulating the heart but also all the other organs and body parts in the heart's zone. Each part of the foot

● Did you know?

Homeodynamics: the physiological processes that maintains internal body systems in a state of equilibrium, whilst undergoing constant changes in the external conditions.

is a different 'reflex area' which connects to a particular part of the body. Reflexologists use their thumbs and fingers to look for areas of tenderness in the reflexes, reading these as a signal that there is a problem in the corresponding part of the body and working that reflex accordingly. Some also look for crystal deposits (a granular texture under the surface of the skin) as proof of a problem area and work the reflexes to remove the build-up of crystals.

Why use the feet?

Eunice Ingham, known as the 'mother' of reflexology to many reflexologists because she developed the therapy, realised that all the nerves in the body ended in the feet. She thus mapped the zones of the body and their contents onto the feet and reflexology was born. Hands can be used but feet are more sensitive because they are usually covered by socks and shoes whereas hands are only protected or gloved when using chemicals and in cold weather.

'Mapping' the feet

When developing the therapy, Ingham produced reflexology charts which mapped the body's anatomy onto the feet and showed how it could be treated using the feet. The charts are similar to maps, with different lines and landmarks that help locate the part of the foot that will help treat the corresponding part of the body. The next section explains and illustrates the different zones and transverse lines which map the feet, before showing how these work on the charts. There are two main mapping tools: the ten longitudinal zones and the transverse, or horizontal zones or guidelines.

The ten zones

The diagram shows the ten zones, running longitudinally (lengthwise) through the body. Each zone roughly

corresponds to a finger/toe, which provides a simple numbering system, and there are five either side of the midline, an imaginary line through the centre of the body. They are all the same approximate width and run back to front as well as head to toe. Just as they 'slice' through the body, they slice through the feet and hands.

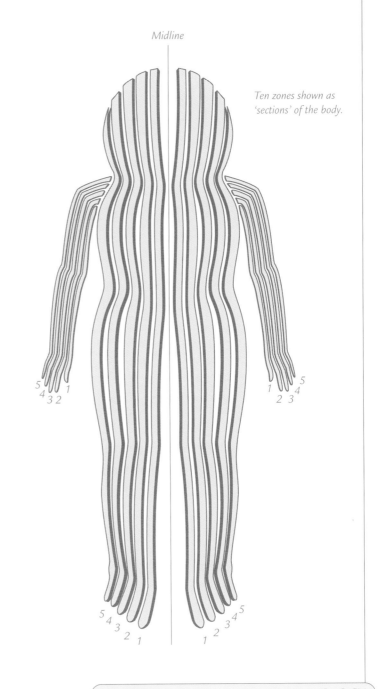

Midline

Ten zones shown as 'sections' of the body.

Transverse zones

Just as there are vertical and horizontal lines on route maps and globes (longitude and latitude) there are also vertical and horizontal lines on foot 'maps'. The horizontal lines, known as transverse lines or zones, help to 'interpret' the zones and 'locate' organs and glands within each one. Two famous reflexology practitioners, Dwight Byers and Hanne Marquardt, have defined these. Byers, nephew of Eunice Ingham, calls them 'Body Relation Guide Lines' whereas Marquardt calls them 'Transverse Zones'.

There are three guidelines or zones:

1. shoulder: this line is placed at the join between the head and the body
2. waist: across the centre of the body
3. pelvic: across the bottom of the torso where it joins the legs, at the level of the hips. The diaphragm line is also classed by some as an additional transverse zone.

Each line has a corresponding line on the foot:

1. the base of the toes (where the phalanges meet the metatarsals): just as the toes represent the head and the rest of the foot represents the body, thus where the toes join the rest of the foot represents where the head joins the rest of the body
2. the centre of the foot, or arch (where the metatarsals meet the tarsal, or ankle bones)
3. the back of the foot, or heel (the tarsals).

How do these lines help locate different parts of the body?

In each transverse section of the foot, reflex areas for particular parts of the body are located. Thus:

- everything in the toe area, above the shoulder line corresponds to everything above the shoulders on the body, i.e. the head and neck area (see area A on diagram opposite)
- everything between the base of the toes and the top of the tarsals, between the shoulder line and waist line, corresponds to everything between the shoulders and waist on the body, i.e.

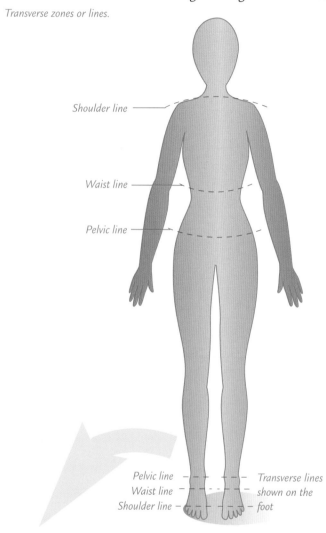

Transverse zones or lines.

Shoulder line

Waist line

Pelvic line

Pelvic line — Transverse lines
Waist line — shown on the
Shoulder line — foot

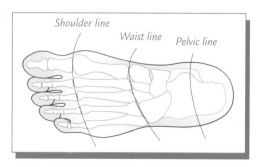

Shoulder line

Waist line   Pelvic line

the heart and lungs, diaphragm and ribs, and stomach and liver (see area B on diagram below)

- everything below the waist line and above the pelvic line corresponds to everything between the waist and pelvic floor, i.e. all the abdominal organs such as the large and small intestine, the kidneys and the bladder (see area C on diagram below).

The relationship between areas of the body and the feet in reflexology.

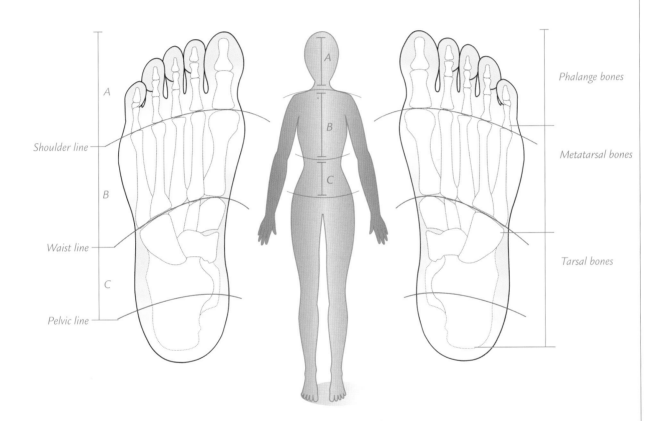

A

Shoulder line

B

Waist line

C

Pelvic line

Phalange bones

Metatarsal bones

Tarsal bones

Connections within a zone

Parts of the body within a certain zone are all linked and can thus affect one another. A blockage or problem in one part of a zone will affect the entire zone. Thus, since the feet are part of the zones (see diagram p.15), by working with them a reflexologist can relieve blockages and release tensions throughout the body. Organs in zone one will be affected by pressure on zone one on the foot or hand. Furthermore, by working the whole of the left foot, the whole of the left side of the body will be affected and vice versa.

THE SPINE AND ITS IMPORTANCE

The central line through the body, its support and nerve network, is the spine. Many reflexologists believe that the feet and spine are closely connected because there are 26 bones in each foot and 26 (individual) bones in the spine and the curves in the spine are similar to those in the feet. Because it runs right through the centre of the body it is represented on the maps of both feet, right and left. The 'spine zone' runs along the whole length of the foot, on the inside and, just as the spine has five different sections, from cervical to coccygeal, so it has five zones for reflexology purposes (see Chapter 5 for more information).

You now know all the location pointers and landmarks to look for when mapping the feet. We can now move on to looking at the complete maps and learning the theory behind why a squeeze of the toe may affect the head.

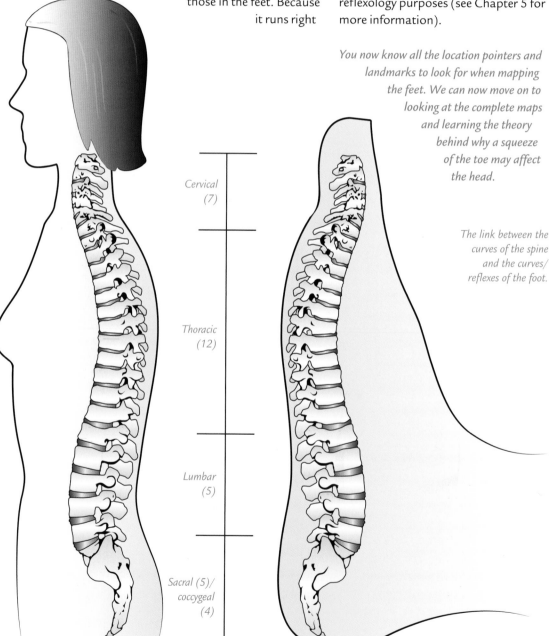

Cervical (7)

Thoracic (12)

Lumbar (5)

Sacral (5)/ coccygeal (4)

The link between the curves of the spine and the curves/ reflexes of the foot.

Foot 'maps'

You now know that reflexology divides the body up into ten vertical zones and three horizontal zones and that within each part of the foot there are reflex areas, i.e. massaging and manipulating a reflex area will positively affect a corresponding area in the body. There are also maps for the hands, which follow the same principles. The charts for the feet and hands, which are standard for use in reflexology, are shown on the following pages and also on a fold out in the back cover of the book .

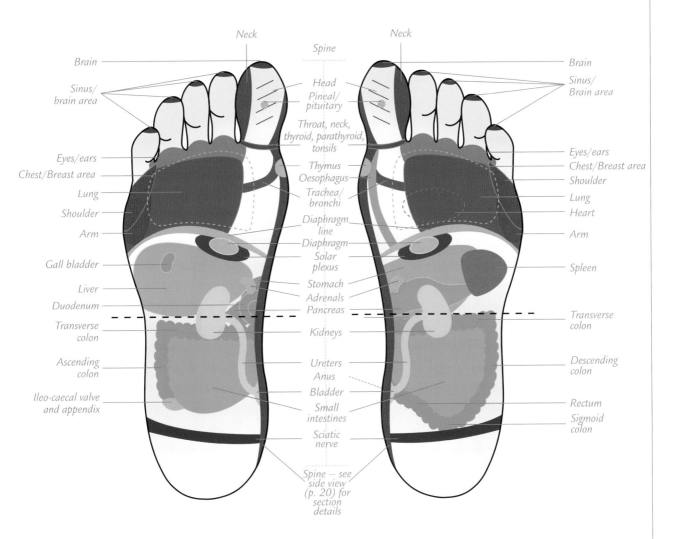

Neck

Spine

Neck

Brain

Sinus/ brain area

Head

Pineal/ pituitary

Brain

Sinus/ Brain area

Throat, neck, thyroid, parathyroid, tonsils

Eyes/ears

Chest/Breast area

Thymus

Oesophagus

Eyes/ears

Chest/Breast area

Lung

Trachea/ bronchi

Shoulder

Shoulder

Diaphragm line

Lung

Arm

Diaphragm

Heart

Solar plexus

Arm

Gall bladder

Stomach

Spleen

Liver

Adrenals

Duodenum

Pancreas

Transverse colon

Transverse colon

Kidneys

Ascending colon

Ureters

Descending colon

Anus

Ileo-caecal valve and appendix

Bladder

Small intestines

Rectum

Sigmoid colon

Sciatic nerve

Spine — see side view (p. 20) for section details

Side views on following page.

Side views of
foot maps.

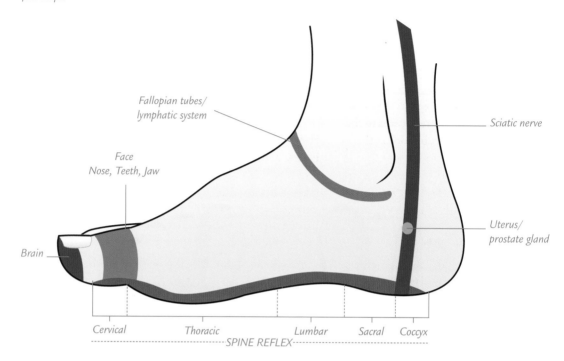

Fallopian tubes/
lymphatic system

Face
Nose, Teeth, Jaw

Sciatic nerve

Brain

Uterus/
prostate gland

Cervical   Thoracic   Lumbar   Sacral   Coccyx
--------------------------------------- SPINE REFLEX ---------------------------------------

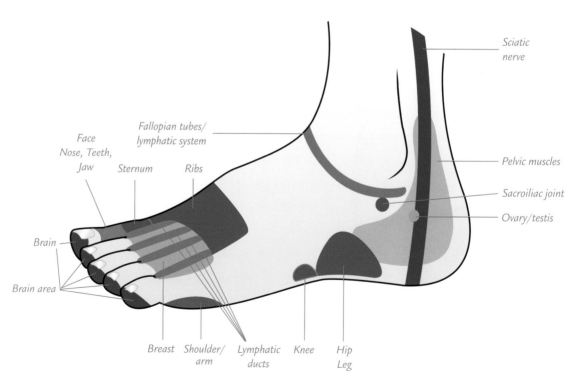

Sciatic
nerve

Fallopian tubes/
lymphatic system

Face
Nose, Teeth,
Jaw   Sternum   Ribs

Pelvic muscles

Sacroiliac joint

Ovary/testis

Brain

Brain area

Breast   Shoulder/   Lymphatic   Knee   Hip
         arm   ducts   Leg

How does information get from a point on the foot map to a point somewhere else in the body?

The areas shown on these maps are known as reflex areas or zones. A reflex area is the relationship between a point on the foot and another area of the body: when a reflex area is stimulated through massage or manipulation the corresponding part of the body is affected. It is not known exactly how the stimulus travels from the reflex area to the corresponding body part but one of the simplest ways to understand the connection is to think of it as energy. It should not be confused with a nerve reflex. If you look at the maps you will see that:

- the toes are the reflex areas for the head and brain area
- the inside heel is the reflex area for the lower spine, the sacrum and coccyx
- the arch of the foot is the reflex area for the abdominal organs such as the small and large intestines.

For example by working all the reflex areas of the left foot, the whole of the left side of the body will be affected and vice versa.

Referral areas

Finally, a word about referral areas. In reflexology each foot is treated like a mirror of the body, reflecting its different parts. However, if the foot or leg is

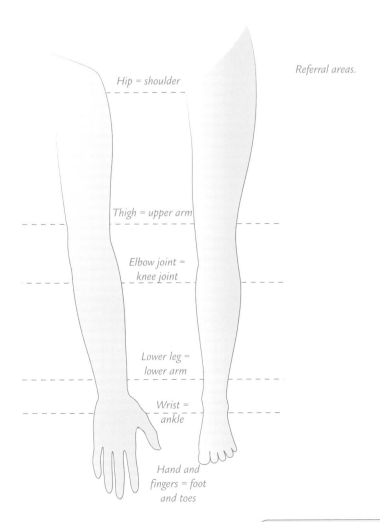

Referral areas.

Hip = shoulder

Thigh = upper arm

Elbow joint = knee joint

Lower leg = lower arm

Wrist = ankle

Hand and fingers = foot and toes

THEORY AND CONCEPT OF REFLEXOLOGY

damaged then the referral areas in the hand and arm can be used. The arm and leg are considered to correspond with each other. Just as the hand has similar reflex areas to the foot, so does the rest of the arm. The easiest way to understand this is to think of the human body as having evolved from a four-legged animal to a biped. Our arms and legs are thus very similar: the wrist is the referral area for the ankle, the elbow is the referral area for the knee, the lower arm is the referral area for the calf and the upper arm is the referral area for the thigh. Referral areas are very useful when there is a problem with a leg or foot because the corresponding area on the arm (e.g. for a broken ankle the wrist would be worked on) can be treated, thus benefiting the injury and helping the healing process. Referral areas are also known as cross reflexes.

The theory of hand treatments

Hand reflexology, though not as common as foot reflexology, can be used in some situations. The hands and feet have very similar anatomy and shape and every part of the feet used in reflexology has an equivalent in the hands. Thus the toes are the fingers, the heel is the wrist, the palm is the sole and the thumb is the big toe. The hands are mapped in the same way as the feet, with reflexes for each part of the body. The hands are not as sensitive as the feet, because they are generally less protected. Thus working some of the deeper reflexes will be harder than on the feet.

Why use the hands?

The hands are used when it is not possible, convenient or suitable to use the feet. For example, someone may have a permanent or temporary impediment to foot reflexology: the loss of a limb, a fracture, sprain or a skin problem. The

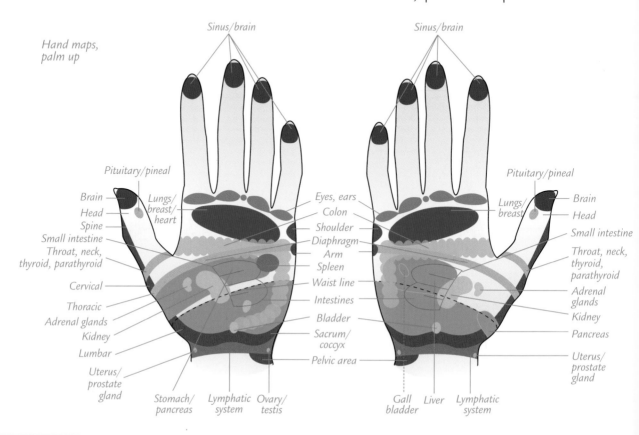

Hand maps, palm up

Sinus/brain

Sinus/brain

Pituitary/pineal
Brain
Head
Spine
Small intestine
Throat, neck, thyroid, parathyroid
Cervical
Thoracic
Adrenal glands
Kidney
Lumbar
Uterus/ prostate gland

Lungs/ breast/ heart

Eyes, ears
Colon
Shoulder
Diaphragm
Arm
Spleen
Waist line
Intestines
Bladder
Sacrum/ coccyx
Pelvic area

Stomach/ pancreas
Lymphatic system
Ovary/ testis

Gall bladder
Liver
Lymphatic system

Pituitary/pineal
Lungs/ breast
Brain
Head
Small intestine
Throat, neck, thyroid, parathyroid
Adrenal glands
Kidney
Pancreas
Uterus/ prostate gland

client may be embarrassed or uncomfortable with someone touching their feet, especially if the treatment is taking place in public such as a hospital ward. The hands are also very useful for self-treatment.

How do you work them?

The same techniques are used on the hands. One hand works whilst the other supports. The thumb is walked across the palms, with the fingers of the same hand used for leverage. When working the top of the hands, especially the areas between the metacarpal bones, the index fingers will give more precise pressure.

Are the reflexes in similar places to those on the feet?

Generally speaking, the reflexes on the feet will be in an equivalent position on the hands. The ten longitudinal zones and the transverse zones can also be mapped on the hands and reflexes which

exist in one zone on the feet will usually be in the same zone on the hands. Reflexes on the toes will be on the fingers, those on the big toe will be on the thumb, those on the ball of the foot will be on the top of the palm, directly below the fingers, those close to the ankle/heel will be close to the wrist. For example, the head and brain reflex on the big toe, is on the thumb. The eyes and ears reflexes, at the base of the toes on the sole of the foot, are at the base of the fingers on the palm of the hand. The lymph and Fallopian tubes reflex, where the top of the foot joins the ankle, are positioned at the join of the top of the hand and wrist.

You now know the theory of reflexology and how it uses the feet or hands to treat the whole body. You also know what reflexes, reflex zones and referral areas are and have the information needed to help you locate all the parts of the body on a foot or hand chart.

Hand maps, palm down

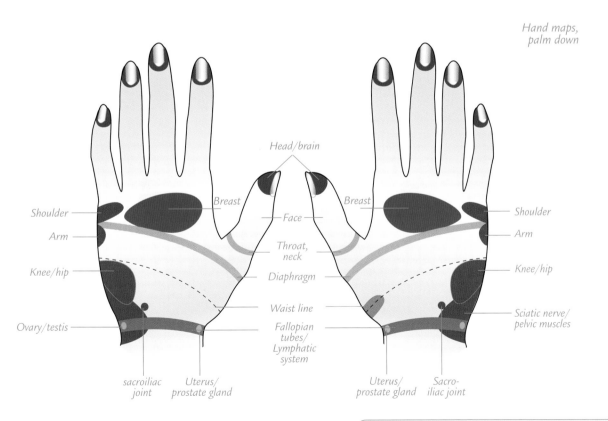

THEORY AND CONCEPT OF REFLEXOLOGY

DON'T FORGET TO LOGIN TO GAIN ACCESS TO YOUR FREE MULTI-MEDIA LEARNING RESOURCES

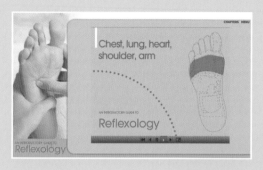

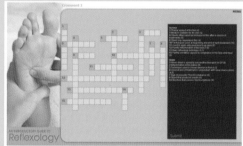

- **IMPROVE YOUR KNOWLEDGE WITH THE INTERACTIVE ANIMATIONS AND DIAGRAMS**

- **TEST YOUR KNOWLEDGE WITH CROSSWORDS**

- **TEST YOUR KNOWLEDGE WITH FILL IN THE GAPS**

AND MUCH MORE!

To login to use these resources visit www.emspublishing.co.uk/reflex and follow the onscreen instructions.

An introductory guide to Reflexology

3 Structure and diseases of hands and feet

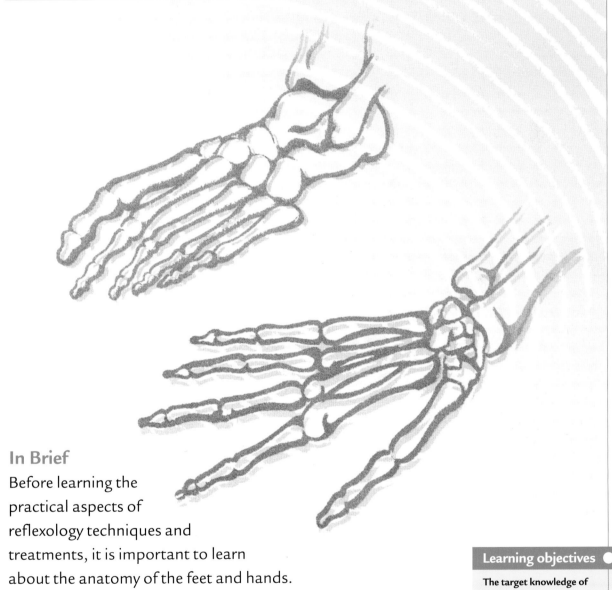

In Brief

Before learning the practical aspects of reflexology techniques and treatments, it is important to learn about the anatomy of the feet and hands. Physical treatments have physical effects and in order to understand these effects it helps to understand the part of the body being treated. This chapter describes the anatomy of the hands and feet as well as the specific problems and diseases which affect them.

STRUCTURE AND DISEASES OF HANDS AND FEET

THE FOOT AND LOWER LEG

The foot's function is to support the weight of the body, to move it forward and lift it in order to make steps and walk.

The skeletal system

The foot and lower leg are part of the appendicular skeleton. This section of the skeleton supports the body's appendages, i.e. the limbs, and attaches them to the torso.

The lower leg

The lower leg has two bones, the tibia and fibula. The tibia, also known as the shin bone, is the thicker of the two. The fibula is parallel to the tibia and is attached to it by ligaments. It is not as important as the tibia in supporting the body which is why the bone is often used for grafting onto other bones elsewhere in the body.

The foot

The foot comprises the ankle, arch or instep and five toes. It has 26 bones: 14 phalanges (toe bones), five metatarsals (the long bones forming the ball and main body of the foot, equivalent to the 'palm' bones in the hand) and seven tarsals (ankle bones).

Each toe has three phalanges bones, apart from the big toe which has only two, and these phalanges join, at the base of each toe, with the metatarsal bones. The metatarsals form the main body of the foot and join with the front row of ankle bones or tarsals — the medial, intermediate and lateral cuneiforms and the cuboid. The other tarsals, the navicular, calcaneus and talus form the back part of the ankle and join with the tibia.

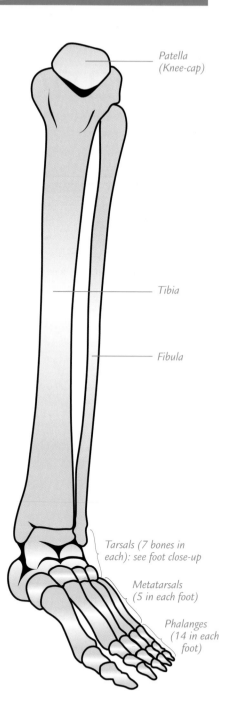

Patella (Knee-cap)

Tibia

Fibula

Tarsals (7 bones in each): see foot close-up

Metatarsals (5 in each foot)

Phalanges (14 in each foot)

Bones of the lower leg and foot

Arches of the feet

There are three arches in each foot:
The medial or inner longitudinal arch
The lateral or outer longitudinal arch
The transversal arch

The arches are maintained by the complex interactions of the bones, ligaments, muscles and tendons. Conditions affecting the arches of the feet alter the weight bearing pattern and capacity of the foot and postural and muscular complications then arise. Irregularities in the foot arches are thought to signify spinal or back problems – Pes planus, where the arch has dropped may indicate lower back pain, and Pes cavus or high arch may indicate spinal problems in the thoracic area.

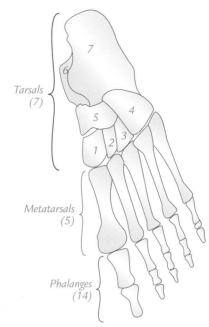

Tarsals
(7)

Metatarsals
(5)

Phalanges
(14)

1. Medial cuneiform
2. Intermediate cuneiform
3. Lateral cuneiform
4. Cuboid
5. Navicular
6. Calcaneum
7. Talus

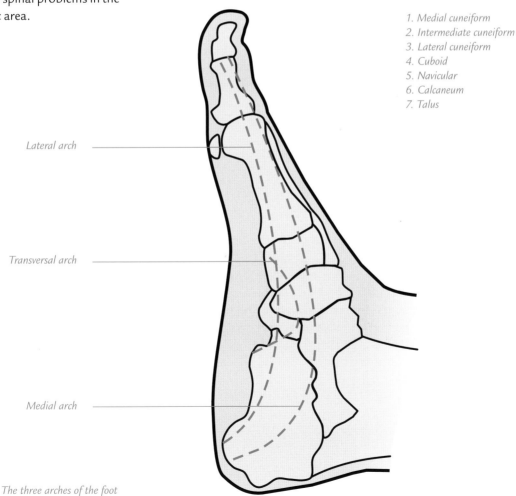

Lateral arch

Transversal arch

Medial arch

The three arches of the foot

The muscular system

Muscles are tissues which attach to other parts of the body, such as bones, to enable movement.

Labels:

1. Gastrocnemius
Position: posterior of the leg; along with the soleus forms the tendon of Achilles
Action: plantarflexes the ankle, flexes the leg at the knee, i.e. moves them up and down, as in walking

2. Soleus
Position: deep and attaches to the gastrocnemius
Action: plantarflexes the ankle

3. Peroneus longus
Position: lateral anterior of leg
Action: plantarflexes the foot, supports the arches and everts the foot, i.e. allows the side of the foot to move up and away from the ground.

4. Peroneus brevis
Position: outer side of the leg attached to the fibula and fifth metatarsal

Action: plantarflexes and everts the foot; gives lateral stability to the ankle.

5. Tibialis anterior
Position: lateral front of lower leg
Action: dorsiflexes and inverts foot.

6. Tibialis posterior
Position: lateral back of lower leg
Action: plantarflexes and inverts the foot.

7. Extensor digitorum longus
Position: anterior aspect of lower leg
Action: extends the toes.

8. Extensor hallucis longus
Position: in big toe
Action: extends toe.

9. Flexor digitorum longus
Position: deep to soleus
Action: flexes the toes, inverts foot.

10. Peroneus tertius
Position: Lateral side of lower leg
Action: Dorsiflexes, everts and abducts foot

11. Digitorum brevis
Position: Lateral aspect of foot
Action: Extends toes

12. Abductor hallucis
Position: Medial side of heel
Action: Flexes and abducts big toe

13. Achilles tendon
Position: Base of Gastrocnemius and Soleus to posterior aspect of Calcaneus
Action: When muscles contract, it plantarflexes foot

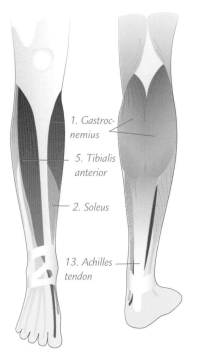

1. Superficial (top) layer

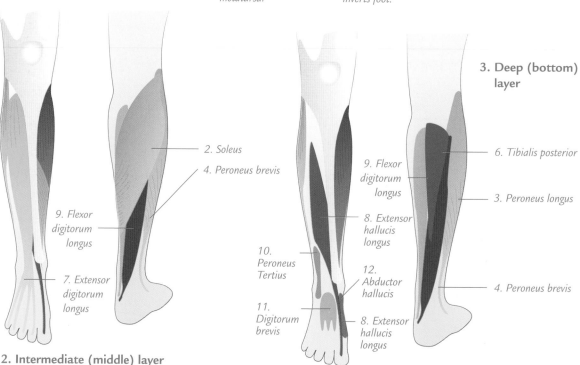

2. Intermediate (middle) layer

3. Deep (bottom) layer

The circulatory or vascular system

The circulatory system is a transport system, comprised of arteries, veins and capillaries, that runs throughout the body. It carries blood, a fluid, connective tissue which is used to distribute food and oxygen and to collect waste and carbon dioxide. The main veins and arteries of the lower leg and foot are shown on the diagrams below.

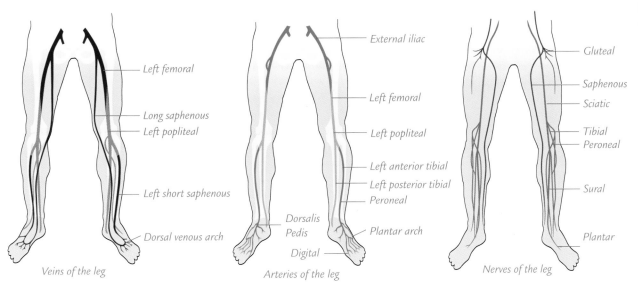

Left femoral

Long saphenous
Left popliteal

Left short saphenous

Dorsal venous arch

Veins of the leg

External iliac

Left femoral

Left popliteal

Left anterior tibial
Left posterior tibial
Peroneal

Dorsalis
Pedis

Plantar arch

Digital

Arteries of the leg

Gluteal

Saphenous
Sciatic

Tibial
Peroneal

Sural

Plantar

Nerves of the leg

The nervous system

The nervous system is the body's communication and instruction network. For the purposes of reflexology it is probably the most important structural system in the body, since there are approximately 7000 nerve endings in the feet, which will be touched by the practitioner's hands and send messages through the whole body from foot to brain. The soothing and stimulating feelings of the massage and manipulation will be transmitted throughout the body by the nervous system. Thus if your feet feel good — warm, relaxed, touched — so will the rest of your body. Soothing the nervous system helps to reduce the symptoms of stress.

You now know the structure of the foot and lower leg.

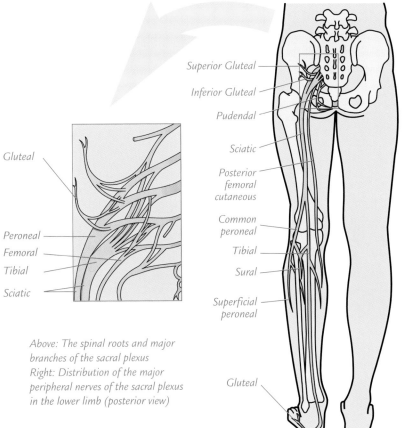

Gluteal

Peroneal
Femoral
Tibial
Sciatic

Superior Gluteal
Inferior Gluteal
Pudendal
Sciatic
Posterior femoral cutaneous
Common peroneal
Tibial
Sural
Superficial peroneal
Gluteal

*Above: The spinal roots and major branches of the sacral plexus
Right: Distribution of the major peripheral nerves of the sacral plexus in the lower limb (posterior view)*

THE LOWER ARM AND HAND

The hands, wrist and lower arm have several functions, including lifting, holding, propelling the body (in walking and running), picking up and carrying. In reflexology they are the referral areas for the feet, ankles and lower legs and they are remarkably similar in structure. They are also used for treatment, either self-help or when the foot cannot be used.

The skeletal system

The hand and arm are constructed in a very similar way to the foot and leg. They are also part of the appendicular skeleton.

The lower arm has two bones: the radius and ulna. They articulate with the humerus (upper arm) bone,

forming the elbow joint and with the upper row of carpal (wrist) bones. The hand has 27 bones: eight carpal (wrist) bones, five metacarpal (palm) bones and 14 phalanges (finger bones). Each finger has three phalanges and each thumb has two. The phalanges join the metacarpals at the base of the fingers and thumb, i.e. the palm of the hand. The metacarpals then articulate with the first row of carpal bones (hamate, capitate, trapezoid and trapezium), which then articulate with the second row of carpal bones (scaphoid, lunate, triquetral and pisiform). The second row of carpals then articulate with the lower arm bones, the radius and ulna.

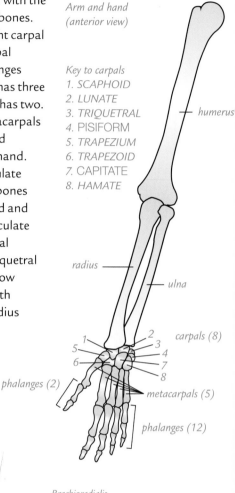

Arm and hand
(anterior view)

Key to carpals
1. SCAPHOID
2. LUNATE
3. TRIQUETRAL
4. PISIFORM
5. TRAPEZIUM
6. TRAPEZOID
7. CAPITATE
8. HAMATE

humerus

radius

ulna

carpals (8)

phalanges (2)

metacarpals (5)

phalanges (12)

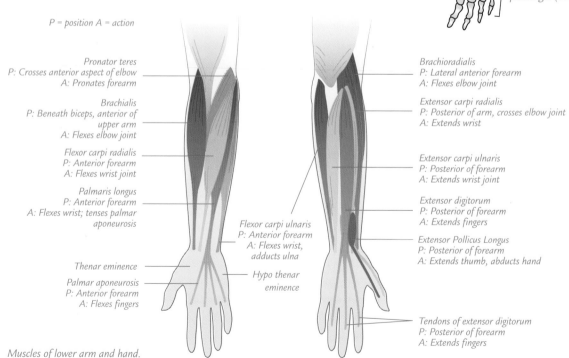

P = position A = action

Pronator teres
P: Crosses anterior aspect of elbow
A: Pronates forearm

Brachialis
P: Beneath biceps, anterior of upper arm
A: Flexes elbow joint

Flexor carpi radialis
P: Anterior forearm
A: Flexes wrist joint

Palmaris longus
P: Anterior forearm
A: Flexes wrist; tenses palmar aponeurosis

Thenar eminence

Palmar aponeurosis
P: Anterior forearm
A: Flexes fingers

Flexor carpi ulnaris
P: Anterior forearm
A: Flexes wrist, adducts ulna

Hypo thenar eminence

Brachioradialis
P: Lateral anterior forearm
A: Flexes elbow joint

Extensor carpi radialis
P: Posterior of arm, crosses elbow joint
A: Extends wrist

Extensor carpi ulnaris
P: Posterior of forearm
A: Extends wrist joint

Extensor digitorum
P: Posterior of forearm
A: Extends fingers

Extensor Pollicus Longus
P: Posterior of forearm
A: Extends thumb, abducts hand

Tendons of extensor digitorum
P: Posterior of forearm
A: Extends fingers

Muscles of lower arm and hand.

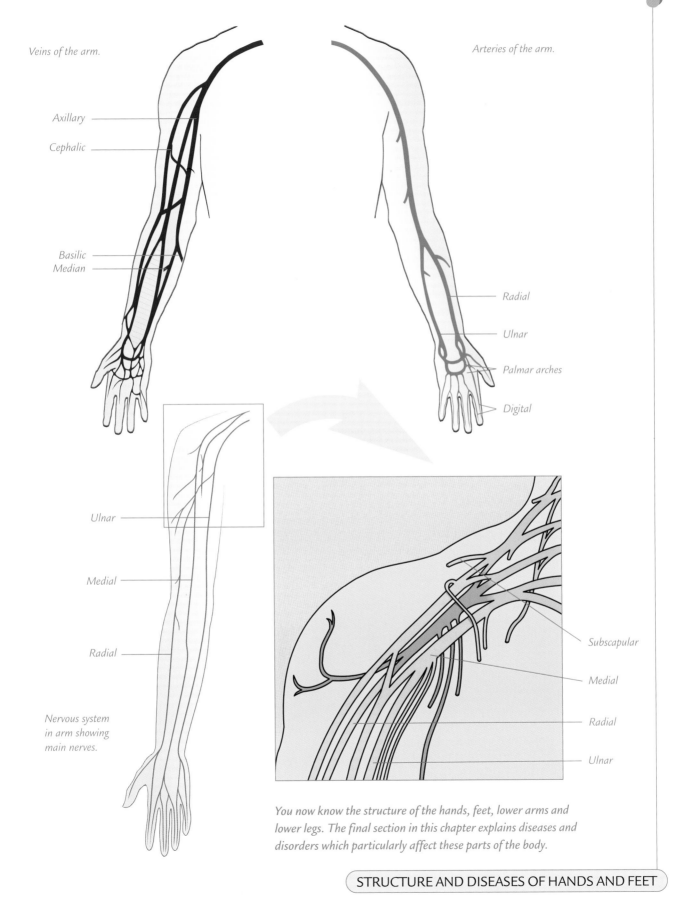

Veins of the arm.

Axillary

Cephalic

Basilic
Median

Arteries of the arm.

Radial

Ulnar

Palmar arches

Digital

Ulnar

Medial

Radial

Nervous system
in arm showing
main nerves.

Subscapular

Medial

Radial

Ulnar

You now know the structure of the hands, feet, lower arms and
lower legs. The final section in this chapter explains diseases and
disorders which particularly affect these parts of the body.

STRUCTURE AND DISEASES OF HANDS AND FEET

DISEASES AND DISORDERS OF THE FEET, HANDS AND NAILS

Anyone who has ever damaged their foot, ankle or toe will know how important and fundamental the feet are to our daily lives. A broken toe can make it impossible to balance or walk and even a bunion or corn can affect a person's wellbeing and balance. The feet support the whole weight of the body and are used constantly in walking, standing and supporting the body. So it is no surprise that such an important part of the body, often mistreated by ill-fitting shoes or poor posture, can be affected by many different disorders and diseases. The following section lists some of the main ones that affect the feet, hands and nails. If the reflexologist suspects contagious infection of the skin or nails, the treatment should be restricted i.e. the hands worked on rather than the feet or the client referred until suitable diagnosis is made. Chronic conditions such as arthritis may be worked upon providing medical or specialist permission has been given for the treatment to go ahead. (see Chapter 7 for further details).

Congenital

Exists at birth, may be inherited.

Eczema

May affect the skin or the nails and can be hereditary or result from excessive contact with chemicals. Skin appears inflamed and rashes may occur. On the nail, multiple irregular ridges, pitting and nail shedding may be evident.

Psoriasis

An inflammatory condition. In the skin, cells excessively reproduce creating silvery scales over red patches, commonly seen on the elbows and knees. On the nails, it causes pitting, ridges, thickening of the nail, and may lead to fungal infections.

Fungal

Fungal infections are often contagious and/or develop in warm, damp parts of the feet . A fungus is a growth which spreads rapidly.

Tinea unguium

Also known as Onychomycosis
Cause: Fungal infection that lives on keratin, contagious
Effect: disfigures nails, causing them to thicken, discolour and separate from the nail bed

Tinea pedis

Also known as athlete's foot.
Cause: a contagious fungal infection that thrives in warmth and moisture; damp, warm places are likely breeding grounds (e.g. swimming pools, gyms, changing rooms); not drying feet properly can make it worse.
Effect: skin starts off red and itchy, then becomes white; Skin may blister, peel or split very painful and contagious.

Viral infections

A virus is a microscopic disease–producing entity which 'lives' in most cells. The common cold is caused by a virus. The virus reproduces itself in the 'host' – and thus in this case can spread rapidly in the human body.

Verrucas (plantar warts)

Cause: Caused by human papillomavirus (HPV)
Effect: small horny tumour on feet. usually with a black spot in the centre. May spread to form clusters. Highly contagious.

Warts

Cause: Caused by human papillomavirus (HPV)
Effect: small horny tumour found on hands and feet. Highly contagious

Arthritis

An inflammation of the joints. Several forms exist: mono-articular arthritis affects one area and poly-arthritis affects several. There are many factors that are thought to cause arthritis or exacerbate in its varied forms – age, weight, genetics, lifestyle, occupation, previous injury.

Gout.

Cause: deposits of uric acid within joint and cartilage

Effect: often manifests as extremely tender/ painful big toe or ankle, severe pain, swelling and warmth in joint(s), skin becomes red and shiny, thought to be genetic and more common in men.

Osteo-arthritis

Cause: may be injury of the joint and/or may be linked to aging.

Effect: chronic arthritis (involving loss of cartilage, deposition of bone tissue around the joints, pain and inflammation) which gradually worsens; particularly affects weight-bearing joints (e.g. ankles, knees, hips).Pain, stiffness and limitations in joint movement may result.

Rheumatoid arthritis

A form of poly-arthritis.

Cause: Thought to be an autoimmune disease. Antibodies are produced that attack tissue surrounding the joints, causing inflammation and damage to the cartilage and bones.

Effect: inflammation of several joints, commonly affects wrists, fingers, feet, ankles and toes although any body joint may be affected.

Hallux rigidus

Cause: damage to nerves; injury to toe; inflammation from arthritis or gout; wear and tear on cartilage.

Effect: joint between big toe and first metatarsal becomes stiff and painful.

Causes pain elsewhere in foot and ultimately difficulty in walking.

Hallux valgus (also known as bunion)

Cause: lateral displacement of the joint of the big toe

Effect: displaced big toe; swelling, pain and discomfort.

Hammer toes

Cause: ill-fitting shoes

Effect: painful, deformed middle toe or toes; often results in corns and nail problems.

Bone/Heel spurs

Cause: bony growth under the heel

Effect: painful; possible difficulty in walking and standing.

Club foot

Talipes equinovarus

Cause: Congenital disorder. One or both feet turn downward and inward.

Effect: Sufferers appear to walk on their ankles rather than their feet. Corrected by surgery and/or the use of remedial splints, plaster casts and physiotherapy.

Pes planus (Flat feet)

Cause: Loss of the medial longitudinal arch of the foot due to developmental problems, degeneration of bones, obesity, poor footwear.

Effect: Flat foot, where the sole is in full contact with the floor, foot pain, associated pain in legs, knees and back

Foot drop

Cause: Inability to raise the front part of the foot due to weakness or paralysis of muscles due to nerve damage, trauma or progressive disorders.

Effect: Results in the sufferer walking abnormally to prevent the foot 'slapping' down. This is known as 'steppage gait'.

Pes cavus (high arch)
Cause: May be hereditary. Feet have a higher than average arch and the toes may appear to be clawed, shortening the feet.
Effect: There may be pain or tenderness in the arch, the feet may be stiff and lack flexibility. Calf pain, knee pain and hip pain may be present. Some sufferers sprain ankles easily. May cause corns and callouses on the soles and 1st and 5th toes.

Plantar fasciitis
Cause: inflammation of connective tissue running from the heel to the ball of the foot
Effect: severe pain which is normally worse in the morning as the tissues contract during sleep.

Bursitis
Cause: inflammation of synovial fluid of a joint, e.g. big toe joint
Effect: inflammation and pain in the affected area.

Nail disorders
The nails of both the feet and hands are useful indicators of general health. Healthy nails are pink, smooth and not split. Any of the following conditions should be noted:

- Pitting, lines and ridges may indicate systemic changes due to ill health, injury, pregnancy, medication, psoriasis, paronychia, false nails, changes in diet.
- Vertical ridges may indicate injury to the matrix, systemic changes due to illness, arthritis.
- Beau's lines are horizontal/transverse ridges that indicate systemic changes as detailed above
- Habit tic are horizontal ridges in the centre of the nail due to the nail being picked, usually as a result of stress

- Blue/purple nails may indicate poor circulation
- Leuconychia (white spots) may indicate trauma, calcium/nutritional deficiencies or air bubbles between the layers of the nail.
- Yellow, white or discoloured nails may indicate fungal infection-onychomycosis, or staining from products such as nail enamel. Vertical streaks in the nails may be due to splinter haemorrhages from trauma to the matrix or fungal infection.
- Curved or concave nails, and conditions such as koilonychia (spoon nails) may be congenital or indicate lack of minerals such as iron, or excessive exposure to chemicals. Onychogryphosis (ram's horn nails) results in the nails becoming claw like. The nails become thick, fibrous and curved over the tip of the toe. This condition is normally caused by trauma from incorrect footwear.
- Flaking, dry or brittle nails may be caused by deficiencies in the diet, poor circulation, arthritis or over exposure to chemicals or water. Lamellar dystrophy is a condition, which causes the nails to flake off, and is often due to repeated contact with water and detergents.
- Dry skin around the nail plate can result in conditions such as pterygium, where the cuticle overgrows. As the nail plate grows forward, the skin is stretched and may tear. Hangnails can occur, appearing as small tears or splits in the cuticle, which can then become infected, resulting in paronychia. Paronychia is a bacterial infection, seen as inflammation and redness of the skin at the base or side of the nail. Pus may be present. Hangnails and whitlows are often seen when the nails are bitten (onychophagy).

- Onychauxis is often seen in older clients. The nails become thick and uneven. It can result from trauma, fungal infections, psoriasis or pressure from footwear. Another condition often seen in elderly clients is onychatrophia. The nails become thin and fragile, splitting easily. This may be due to chronic conditions such as diabetes, poor circulation, arthritis or trauma to the matrix.
- Onychocryptosis (Ingrowing toenails) is caused when the nails grow into the surrounding skin, usually as a result of poor toenail trimming. It causes pain and infection and may be remedied by removing the source of pressure. Avoid the area until healed.
- Onycholysis results in the nail plate lifting from the nail bed and is often seen as a white area. It is caused by fungal or bacterial infections, trauma, medication or psoriasis.
- Onychia – inflammation of the nail bed resulting from bacterial infection.

Skin disorders
Abrasions
Cause: Damage to the skin caused by contact with a rough surface.
Effect: Skin becomes thin as the epidermis is worn down, usually by friction. Abrasions may be superficial or deep.

Allergies
Cause: Exposure to substances such as chemicals or food that the body has sensitivity to.
Effect: Can result general skin reactions such as urticaria, inflammation or dermatitis, which may also affect the nails.

Bruises
Cause: Trauma to skin or nails resulting in damage to blood vessels.

Effect: Discoloured areas of skin or nail as blood pools in the tissues due to capillary damage. These vary in colour from dark blue to yellow as initial trauma then healing takes place. In the nail, bruising may result in the loss of the nail plate, depending on the area of trauma.

Callouses
Cause: poor posture and poorly-fitting shoes
Effect: thickened hard skin often over large area of the foot.

Chilblains
Cause: Excessive cold causes damage to the capillaries of the extremities. Usually occur in the toes but can also affect the fingers, face and nose.
Effect: Lesions develop that are red, swollen and itchy. They are extremely painful and may be felt as a burning sensation. The skin may dry out and crack, leading to further infection.

Cuts
Cause: Trauma to the skin
Effect: Open wounds exposing the skin and body to infection; small cuts may result in minor damage and bleeding, larger wounds may bleed excessively and require medical intervention i.e. stitches.

Corns
Cause: ill-fitting shoes and/or poor posture put pressure on skin causing inflammation
Effect: skin reacts with the inflammation and the cells become impacted; constant pressure on the same area may produce a cone called a corn; removing the source of pressure helps relieve the problem.

Heel fissures
Cause: dry, thickened skin
Effect: cracks in the skin of the heel; may become infected.

Loss of skin sensation
Cause: Conditions such as diabetes may cause damage to sensory nerves
Effect: Loss of skin sensation; the inability to detect pressure, heat, cold and pain.

Diabetes
Cause: Endocrine disorder affecting blood glucose levels
Effect: Clients with diabetes often have dry skin. Poor blood flow and imbalances in blood glucose results in poor wound healing. Simple conditions such as blisters may develop into serious infections. If left untreated, infections can result in limb amputation. Sufferers may also experience nerve damage (diabetic neuropathy), which leads to loss of sensation and the risk of damage from trauma.

Conditions specific to hands
Carpal tunnel syndrome
Cause: compression of the median nerve as it enters palm of hand; space between carpal bones is a tunnel hence the name
Effect: debilitating pain, especially in index and middle fingers; intermittent numbness and muscle weakness.

RSI: repetitive strain injury
Cause: constant keyboard work at computers; any job involving lots of wrist flexion, prolonged finger extension
Effect: wrist pain, swelling and numbness.

You now know the structure of the hands, feet and lower limbs and some of the diseases and disorders which affect them.

4 Techniques

In Brief

This chapter explains the different techniques that are used in reflexology. There are two types of technique: relaxation and pressure. Those listed here are the main ones used and with practice and experience a reflexologist will develop routines which combine them. The person receiving treatment is referred to as the client.

Learning objectives ●

The target knowledge of this chapter is:
● relaxation techniques
● pressure techniques
● leverage.

THE HANDS OF THE REFLEXOLOGIST

Reflexology uses the hands in a particular way. For the purpose of this chapter it is important to know that there is usually a support hand, which holds the foot being treated and a working hand. Sometimes both hands are working and sometimes both are holding. Generally, the support or holding hand is used to keep the foot stable, protecting the foot being worked from excessive pressure and pinching, maintaining client contact and adequate pressure, providing accessibility through stretch of the foot allowing accurate assessment of reflex points and it acts a base for leverage of the working hand. Correct positioning and use of both the working and support hands are essential if the therapist is to avoid work-related overuse injuries like repetitive strain. The reflexologist's hands should be kept clean and free of any contagious disorders. Nails should be short, trimmed and clean and nail enamel/varnish should not be worn. Reflexology is not generally performed with creams or oils, but other mediums such as talc, corn starch and liquid talc may be used depending on clients' skin type/texture. Creams are often used at the end of the treatment during the foot massage to soften the skin. Therapists who are also qualified in aromatherapy may like to use carrier oils or creams and essential oils to finish a treatment and moisturise any areas of dry skin. If using creams or oils care must be taken to ensure that any excess product is removed and that the client does not slip, so socks or shoes must be worn immediately after the treatment.

RELAXATION TECHNIQUES

If you think about reflexology as a workout for the feet as well as the rest of the body, then it is obvious that in order for the feet and body to benefit as much as possible they must be relaxed and warmed up. This is where relaxation techniques come in. They are used at the beginning and end of a reflexology treatment, preparing the feet before the treatment and 'slowing them down' at the end. The techniques all involve gentle movements and stretches, loosening any tension and stiffness, making the foot and ankle more malleable and thus ready for the pressure techniques of the next stage.

Position of the reflexologist
One of the dangers of being a reflexologist is that most treatment is carried out from a sitting position and this can cause postural problems for the therapist. Throughout a session, the

reflexologist should be sitting, feet flat on the floor and spine relaxed, with the client's feet and face in full view and feet at the level of the reflexologist's shoulders. Chapter 7 explains this in more detail.

Greeting (meeting) the feet
The first contact with the client's feet will set the tone for the whole treatment. Any

relaxed especially if it is their first experience of reflexology. This technique is called 'greeting' because it introduces the client's feet to the therapist's hands.

rough, uncomfortable or hasty contact may have an adverse effect on the client, making them feel tense rather than

To greet the feet:
- take hold of both feet at the same time
- keep holding the feet and remain still in this position for a few minutes
- keep the touch firm and positive.

WARM UP

Ankle stretch

This is a technique that follows on well from greeting the feet because the reflexologist can slide the hands fluidly from holding the feet to holding the ankles. This technique allows a full stretch of the backs of the legs and upper body and relaxes the Achilles tendon as well as the rest of the ankle.

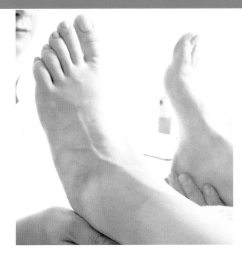

To stretch the ankles:
- with the palms of the hands, hold the backs of both legs just above the ankles
- still holding the legs, gently lean away from the feet and the client for a couple of seconds: this stretches the ankles and legs

- after a couple of seconds, still holding the legs, lean towards the client — this relaxes the ankles and legs
- repeat this sequence a few times without losing contact, all the time maintaining a steady and gentle rhythm.

Effleurage

A gentle stroking movement that helps to relax the feet. Effleurage is a technique often used in massage:

- massage the entire foot with the palms and fingers of each hand, using stroking movements up and along the top of the foot to the ankles and lower leg then down around the ankle and heel, along the soles towards the toes
- repeat several times on each foot.

Back and forth slapping

This technique helps to loosen and relax the metatarsal area:

- put palms of the hands either side of the metatarsal area of the sole of the foot
- move hands quickly back and forth on either side of the foot as if you were pushing the sides of the foot up then down
- try not to rub: the aim is to loosen the bones and any tension
- repeat with the other foot and then the ankles
- once this technique has been mastered it can be used as a continuous up and down movement, starting at the metatarsals then moving down the whole foot to the ankle and then back up the foot.

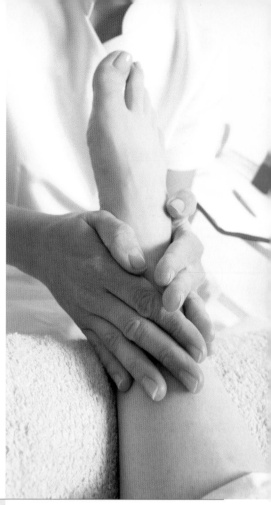

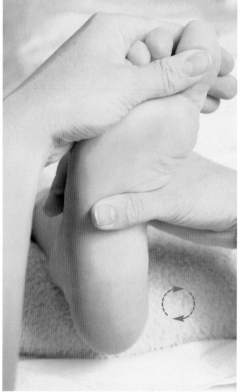

Ankle rotation

This technique helps relax and stretch the ankle. Once mastered it works well as the next step after the ankle stretch:

- place the support hand palm face up under the ankle; place the palm of the working hand on the ball of the foot in the metatarsal area and wrap the fingers up and over the toes
- use the working hand to rotate the metatarsal area/ball of the foot in an oval thus making a circle with the foot
- use more pressure at the beginning of the circle and less at the end
- this can also be done with the support hand palm face down on the top of the ankle and the working hand around the top of the toes.

Toe rotation

This relaxes and stretches each toe individually:

- use the support hand to hold the foot around the ball (metatarsal) area with thumb on the ball and fingers wrapped around the top of the foot (sometimes the support hand is held around the toes that are not being worked on, to separate them from the 'worked' toe)
- take a toe and hold the base with the thumb and index finger of the working hand
- stretch the toe away from the foot
- move the toe around its joint, side to side then in a circle in both directions
- pull the fingers of the working hand along the toe, from the base to the tip, massaging and stretching it as you move along
- repeat with all the toes.

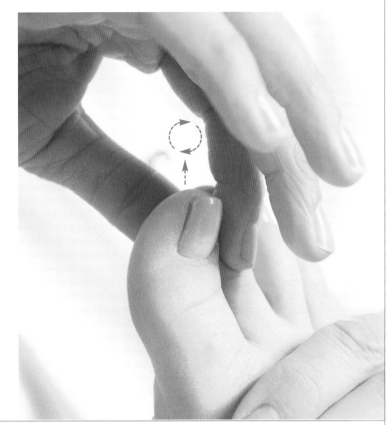

Metatarsal manipulation

This technique stretches and relaxes both the top of the foot and the ball:

- place the support hand palm down over the top of the foot in the metatarsal area, wrapping fingers around the side if necessary
- make the working hand into a fist and put the knuckles (the flat surface formed by the fingers' first phalanges) against the ball of the foot
- lean towards the foot thus putting pressure on the sole/ball of the foot, keeping the support hand's grip quite relaxed (the weight of the reflexologist's body, not a tight grip, should provide the pressure)
- lean away slightly from the foot with the fist, keeping contact, and simultaneously squeeze the metatarsals with the support hand

thus gently pushing the metatarsals against the fist and curling in the toes
- repeat a few times with each foot
- this technique can be combined with kneading.

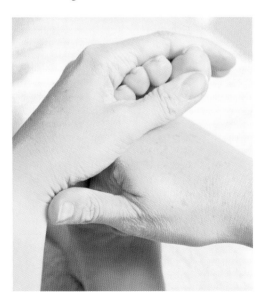

Kneading

This technique is very similar to metatarsal manipulation:

- place the support hand palm down over the top of the foot in the metatarsal area
- make the working hand into a fist and put the knuckles (the flat surface formed by the fingers' first phalanges) against the ball of the foot
- apply gentle pressure with both hands
- circle the fist around the ball of the foot, applying gentle pressure as if kneading dough
- circle in each direction a couple of times on each foot.

Diaphragm release

The diaphragm is often tense which affects the whole body. This technique helps it to relax:

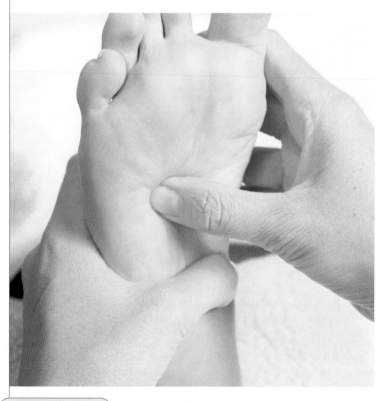

- place the support hand palm down over the top of the foot in the metatarsal area, wrapping fingers around the side if necessary
- press the thumb of the working hand into the centre of the diaphragm line (see diagram) which is at the edge of the ball of the foot above the arch
- use the support hand to gently squeeze the metatarsals towards the working hand, thus curling in the toes
- use gentle pressure in both hands, squeezing the metatarsals and toes with the support hand and pressing in with the thumb of the working hand
- relax then move the thumb along the diaphragm line and repeat
- keep repeating the sequence along the line towards the outside (little toe side) of the foot
- change hands so that the support hand is now the working hand and repeat the sequence, this time from the centre to the inside (big toe side)
- repeat on the other foot.

Spinal twist

As explained in Chapter 2, the curves of the foot are very closely linked to the curves of the spine. This technique loosens the whole foot as well as tension in the vertebrae of the spine:

- place both hands together, palms down, on the inside edge of the foot with the join of the hands at the level of the waist line (see diagram)
- the index fingers should be touching and the thumbs placed on the bottom of the foot (thus holding the foot almost as if it was a sandwich)
- keeping all the fingers of both hands together, rotate the hand nearest the toes back and forth over the inside edge of the foot; the hand nearest the heel should stay as still as possible
- repeat this movement several times
- move the two hands together along the foot towards the toes to an 'untwisted' part of the foot's curve
- repeat the sequence
- continue the moving along the foot and the twisting back and forth until the toe-side (or front) hand is over the toes
- repeat on the other foot.

Wringing

This works in the same way as the spinal twist, but both hands work at the same time.

- place both hands around the foot, palms down with the fingers wrapped around the sides of the foot and the thumbs underneath the sole
- gently twist in opposite directions working up the foot and then back down
- repeat on the other foot

Diaphragm deep breathing

This is recommended for use at the end of a treatment session because it creates a deep feeling of calm and relaxation:

- hold both feet as if greeting the feet
- place the thumbs of both hands onto the diaphragm line at the solar plexus reflex (see diagram p.19)
- ask the client to take a deep breath and hold it for a few seconds and as they do so use both thumbs to apply pressure to the reflex and gently push the feet towards the client
- as they breathe out release the pressure and let the feet move back
- repeat the sequence a few times.

TECHNIQUES

PRESSURE TECHNIQUES

There are four main pressure techniques which involve placing pressure on the reflex areas on the feet, usually using the thumb. The index finger is used when more precision is required.

The support hand position for pressure techniques
The main positions for the support hand in this part of the treatment are as follows:
- the fingers are wrapped around the toes and the top of the foot with the surface of the thumb touching the surface of the big toe or little toe (depending on which foot is being treated and whether the reflexologist is left- or right-handed), and the toes are pulled gently back away from the sole, thus pushing the bottom of the foot out slightly ready for treatment; the heel of the hand (the base of the palm just before the hand joins the wrist) should be positioned against the side of the foot at the level of the metatarsals
- when working on individual toes, the support hand can be used to hold the other toes away from the toe being treated
- the support hand can be placed under the foot, holding it and allowing it to relax for a particular part of the treatment.

Thumb-walking
The thumb is the most important digit in reflexology because walking it across the foot forms the basis of this treatment. It is used to put pressure on reflex areas.

Finding the right position
The best way to find the right position for reflexology is by placing a hand, palm face down, on a flat surface. The thumb naturally rests at a slightly different angle

to the fingers with the side, rather than the pad (fleshy part directly under the nail) against the surface. It is this side, particularly the tip, that is of most use in reflexology.

Walking the thumb
With your hand still on the flat surface, bend the thumb at the first joint and move it forward, making sure that the thumb remains bent. The side edge of the thumb should remain in contact with the surface. Notice how it takes the rest of the hand with it. In thumb-walking, the joint remains bent and the edge is used to press down on the surface of the foot. However, it is not used for a random stroll over the sole! The thumb is moved across the foot in order to put pressure on particular reflex areas, one after the other, in a continuous fluid movement. In order for this technique to have an effect it needs to be combined with leverage.

Leverage
Leverage is the pressure provided by the rest of the working hand as the thumb walks. It is quite difficult to have any effect without it. Try this to see how it works:
- place the thumb of one hand (called the working hand) into the palm of the other (the treated hand) and prevent the rest of the working hand's fingers from touching the treated hand

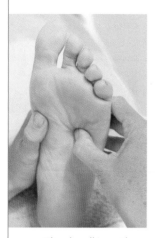

Thumb-walking with thumb bent at first joint.

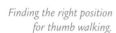

Finding the right position for thumb walking.

- now try thumb-walking across the palm of the treated hand, keeping the fingers away. Is it easy or difficult to apply pressure?
- now try the same process but this time wrap the working hand's fingers around the back of the treated hand. If done properly, it should now be much easier to apply pressure to the palm of the treated hand.

Finger-walking

Finger-walking is the same as thumb-walking: the application of pressure to reflex areas but this time using the index finger. Leverage now comes from the opposite force of the thumb (try the above exercise replacing the working thumb with an index finger). It is used when more precision is required on certain reflexes, provided by the narrower side of a finger.

Focusing on one point

In some cases more pressure will be required at a particular point. In this instance the pressure is slowly reapplied to the same point by moving the thumb/finger as follows:

- use the support hand to hold the foot
- press onto a reflex and point with the thumb/finger in its usual walking position
- instead of edging forward by bending the thumb joint, ease the pressure by gently lifting the thumb away backwards and then push it forwards again onto the same reflex point
- the thumb should not slide across the surface but gently move off backwards and then push forwards to reapply pressure, moving the tissue of the foot as it does so
- this should be a fluid movement.

Pivoting on a point

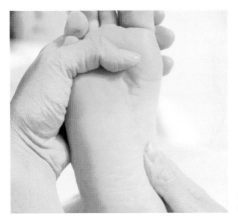

Pivot on kidney and adrenal

This technique is also used to apply extra pressure to a particular area:

- the foot should be held across the toes by the support hand (see above)
- the thumb of the working hand should rest on the reflex area needing treatment
- with the support hand pull the foot onto the thumb of the working hand thus increasing the pressure at the point where the thumb is
- move the working thumb around in a rotation
- move the support hand away to release the pressure
- repeat several times.

Hook

This technique is used to apply pressure to small areas.

- using the four fingers of the working hand for leverage, apply pressure with the thumb to a specific point.
- pull thumb back slightly, do not slip off point but maintain pressure.
- release pressure and continue

Other techniques used during a reflexology treatment may include:-

Rocking – rocking the bent thumb backwards and forwards over a specific point

Finger rolling – useful for treating areas like the tips of the toes, rolling the finger backwards and forwards over a point.

Rotating – similar to pin pointing or focussing on one point but maintaining pressure during the rotation.

You now know how to relax the feet and how to support and apply pressure to reflex areas, the basis of reflexology.

Important points to remember

- finger and thumbnails should be kept short, trimmed and clean at all times; no nail enamel/varnish should be worn
- the first joint of thumb/finger should remain bent
- the movement of thumb- and finger-walking should be smooth and fluid, providing a steady pressure not an intermittent or erratic sensation, whether moving within the same reflex areas or changing to a new one
- the thumb/finger should remain in contact with the foot whilst working
- rubbing the skin is not the same as applying pressure
- the support hand can either be wrapped around the toes as explained above, resting gently over the top of the foot or supporting the heel/ankle
- the thumb/finger always moves forwards, not backwards or sideways
- these techniques can be used for foot or hand treatments
- whilst using any of these techniques the reflexologist should watch the client for signs of possible discomfort
- the reflexologist should maintain a relaxed but upright posture and be aware of any areas of possible tension in their own body.

REFLEXOLOGY ROUTINE

Once the consultation is completed, the therapist may then work through the routine:

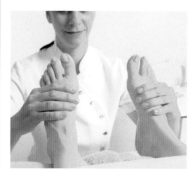

1) Centre self

2) Reading the feet

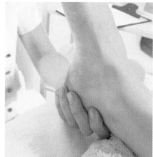

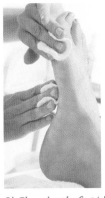 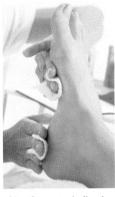   

3) Cleansing the feet/checking for contraindications   **4) Greet feet prior to commencing full treatment** - *Apply powder & wrap foot*

5) Warm up massage

To warm up each foot:

 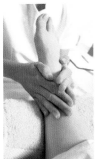    

6 x effleurage

Thumb knead metatarsals   *Circling around tarsals*

   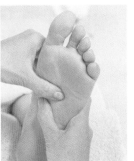

Circling toes   *3 x Cross frictions on sole*

TECHNIQUES

 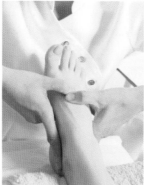  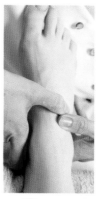 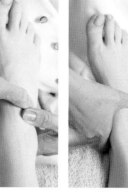

Thumb knead metatarsals *Circling around tarsals*

To warm up each foot continued:

  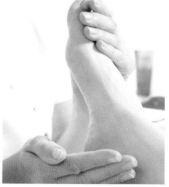

3 x ulnar scraping

 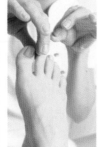 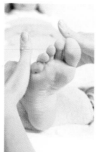 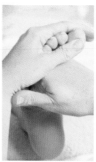 

Picking on toes *Whipping on toes* *Knuckle solar plexus*

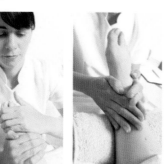  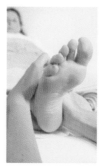  

6 x effleurage

REFLEXOLOGY

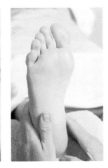
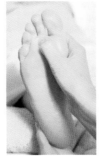
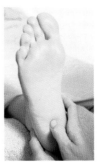

How to find the correct head position

6) Thumb walk zones 5 to 1 (first foot) sole first and then top of foot

All points noted must be charted as the therapist works through the routine.
Maintain contact with client with one hand whilst marking foot chart.

7) Routine
Chest, lung, heart, shoulder, arm

Thumb walk chest and lung area (from diaphragm to neck, shoulder line)   *Thumb walk diaphragm*

Rotations on diaphragm line   *Lung Press – knuckle*

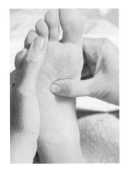
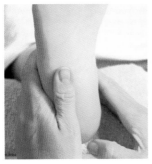

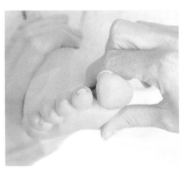

Thumb walk heart   *Thumb walk shoulder and arm*   *Finger walk front of foot (5 Zones) towards ankle*

TECHNIQUES

Head/sinuses

  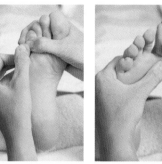  

Thumb walk 5 zones of big toe *Thumb walk other toes x 2 each* *Finger walk down front of toes x 2 each*

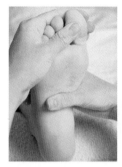 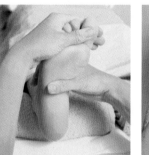 

Rotate all toes together *Hook on pituitary, hook on pineal body -*

Neck, eyes/ears, thyroid, parathyroids

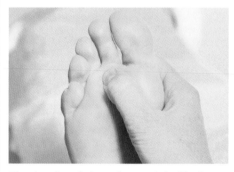  

Thumb walk neck, base of toes and shoulder line *Thumb walk thyroids and parathyroids*

Spine/back

  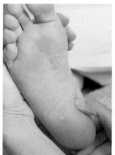 

Thumb walk up spine

REFLEXOLOGY

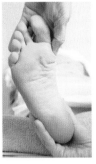    

Thumb walk down spine

Rotate on sacroiliac joint

Finger walk front (middle back)

The abdominal area

    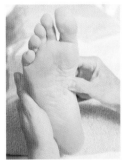

Thumb walk whole area – waist to diaphragm

Thumb walk liver, gall bladder, stomach, pancreas and duodenum – right foot

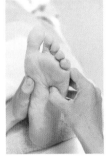 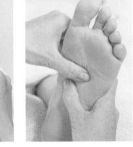 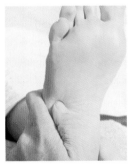 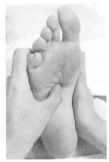 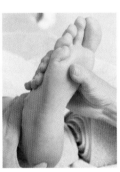

Thumb walk spleen, stomach and pancreas – left foot

Pivot on gall bladder – right foot only

Thumb walk whole area – heel to waistline

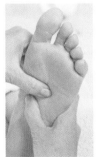  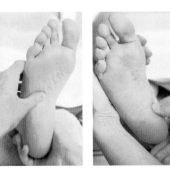 

Thumb walk on diagonal to cover ascending, transverse and descending colon,

small intestine, ileo-caecal valve and appendix

Thumb walk bladder, ureter, kidney and adrenal

Pivot on kidney and adrenal

TECHNIQUES

Leg, knee, hip and sciatic nerve

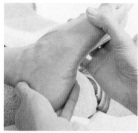
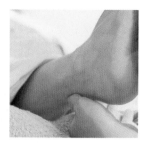

*Thumb walk leg, knee,
hip and lower back*

Thumb walk down sciatic nerve

Reproductive/Lymphatic area

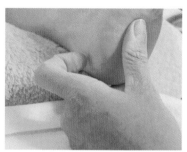

Finger walk up sciatic nerve

Rotate ankle each way

Thumb walk uterus/prostate/pelvic muscles

Thumb walk fallopian tube area

Rotate thumb into hollows at lymph/groin area

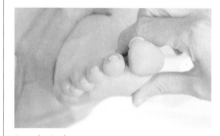
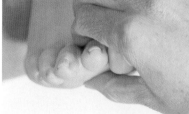
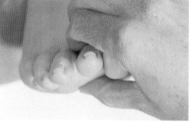

Lymphatic ducts

Ankle jiggle

Cool down massage – light stroking over foot

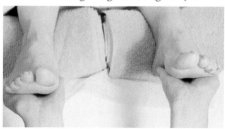

Hold to finish

Repeat routine on the other foot

Relaxation

*Hold both feet at the
same time
Energise – visualisation
Disconnect – palms down
Cover feet with towels*

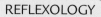

REFLEXOLOGY

5 Application of techniques to the body

In Brief

Each part of the body has a reflex area on the feet and hands. Like the rest of the body, these are all interconnected and working one will benefit others. However, it is useful to remember which reflexes refer to which part of the body and which conditions benefit from working particular reflexes. This chapter details the reflex areas for each body system starting with the skeleton. (You may find it useful to fold out the maps in the back cover to use throughout this chapter.)

Learning objectives

The target knowledge of this chapter is:
- the position of reflex areas for each body system
- the function of reflex areas for each body system.

THE POSITION OF REFLEXES

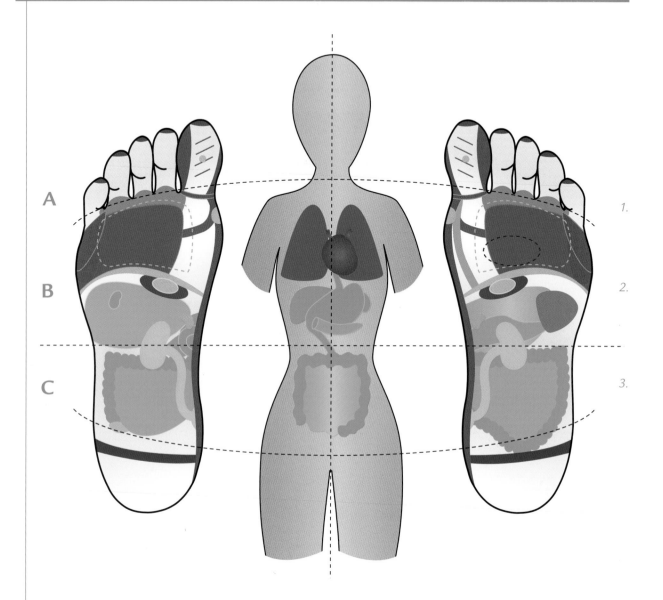

A

B

C

1.

2.

3.

1. Most reflexes for the head and neck are in the toes.

2. Reflexes for the chest are found between the shoulder line and waist line (base of toes to middle of arch).

3. Reflexes for the abdomen are found between the waist line (middle of arch) and the pelvic line (the heel).

You will notice that the position of the reflexes on the soles of the feet are very similar to the position of the organs they represent in the body. Thus, reflexes for the head and face are in the tip of the foot (the toes) and those for the pelvis and lower body are in the heel. Parts of the body with a right and left (kidneys, lungs) will have two reflex areas, one on each foot. It is helpful when learning the position of reflexes to always think of the foot as a mirror of the body (see diagram) because then it becomes easier to locate reflexes.

The illustrations below show all the different reflexes on the feet. These are the foot 'maps' (see also the pull-out chart in the back cover of the book) and they are at the heart of reflexology practice. Each colour represents a system, all of which are detailed separately in this chapter. Many systems overlap so that working one system will also benefit another and it is rare to try and work just the skeletal system or just the lymphatic system. A particular system may be worked more thoroughly but most treatments treat the whole person and thus the whole foot.

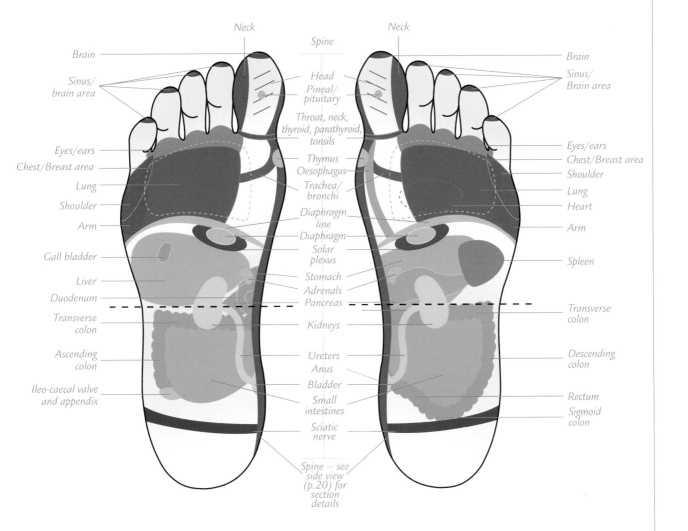

Neck — Spine — Neck

Brain — Brain

Sinus/brain area — Head — Sinus/Brain area

Pineal/pituitary

Throat, neck, thyroid, parathyroid, tonsils

Eyes/ears — Thymus — Eyes/ears
Chest/Breast area — Oesophagus — Chest/Breast area
Lung — Trachea/bronchi — Shoulder
Shoulder — Lung
Arm — Diaphragm line — Heart
Diaphragm — Arm
Gall bladder — Solar plexus — Spleen
Liver — Stomach
Duodenum — Adrenals
Pancreas
Transverse colon — Kidneys — Transverse colon
Ascending colon — Ureters — Descending colon
Anus
Ileo-caecal valve and appendix — Bladder — Rectum
Small intestines — Sigmoid colon
Sciatic nerve
Spine — see side view (p.20) for section details

APPLICATION OF TECHNIQUES TO THE BODY

THE SKELETAL SYSTEM

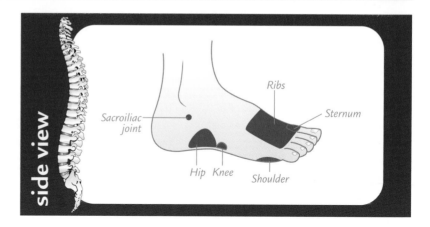

side view

Sacroiliac joint

Ribs

Sternum

Hip Knee Shoulder

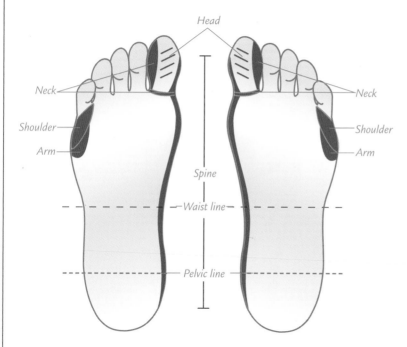

Head

Neck

Shoulder

Arm

Neck

Shoulder

Arm

Spine

Waist line

Pelvic line

On the diagram above you can see all the relevant reflexes for treating the skeleton and associated parts of the body (e.g. tendons that attach muscles to bones). We will work down the body from top to bottom.

Reflex for the head and neck
Where is it?
The reflex area for the head and neck is the big toe. The head is represented by the fleshy part and the neck by the inner edge of the toe (the edge that touches

the second toe) and a narrow strip around the base of the toe.
Why work it?
A rotation of the big toe corresponds to rotating the neck. Working this reflex helps neck and head problems such as stiffness, tension and headaches. It is close

to the spinal reflex and working either one will benefit the other. In the hand the reflex area for the head and neck is the thumb down to the base of the thumb.

Reflex for the spine
Where is it?
The spine reflex area is the inside edge of each foot from toe to heel. For the purposes of reflexology the curves of the spine match the curves of the foot. The reflex has five different sections and each one corresponds to the relevant section of the spine:

- **cervical**: the cervical vertebrae are at the top of the spine and the corresponding reflex area is at the side of the foot, from the tip of the big toe to the base, on the outside edge

- **thoracic**: there are 12 thoracic vertebrae forming the longest part of the spine and the corresponding reflex area is the longest spine zone on the foot, from the base of the big toe to the base of the ball of the foot

- **lumbar**: just as the lumbar vertebrae form the lower arch of the back so the lumbar zone on the foot is the arch: from the base of the ball to the start of the inside heel

- **sacral**: the sacral are just before the end of the spine and the corresponding reflex area is just before the end of the foot: from the start of the inner heel to the middle of the heel

- **coccygeal**: the coccygeal vertebrae are at the bottom of the spine and at the bottom of the reflexology map: from the mid-heel to the back of the foot.

Why work it?

Working the different parts of the spine affects the whole body since it supports the whole body mechanically and is also the communication network for the nervous system. It thus helps not only physical stiffness and tension (especially in the back, neck and head) but also nervous and related disorders. The spine reflex is also closely associated with the head, neck, hip and elbow reflexes so working any one of these will benefit the others.

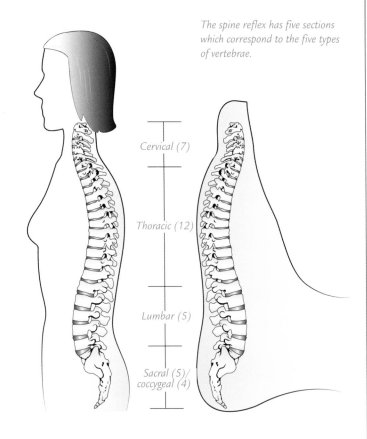

The spine reflex has five sections which correspond to the five types of vertebrae.

Cervical (7)

Thoracic (12)

Lumbar (5)

Sacral (5)/
coccygeal (4)

Reflex for the shoulder and shoulder girdle
Where is it?

The reflex area for the shoulder girdle (which includes the scapulae and collar bones) is on the outside of the sole, just at the base of the fifth toe.

Why work it?

Working the shoulder reflex helps stiffness in this area, or frozen shoulder. It is also closely associated with the arm and elbow reflex so working it will benefit these others and vice versa.

Reflexes for the arm and elbow
Where are they?

Just as the arms are below the shoulders, so the arm reflexes are below those for the shoulder.

Why work them?

Working these reflexes benefits the arm and elbow, relieving problems such as tennis elbow, as well as the shoulder, neck and hand.

Reflex for the sternum and ribs
Where is it?

As we move down the skeleton we reach the thoracic cage, consisting of the sternum and ribs. The reflex area for these bones is on the top of the foot not the sole. The sternum is directly below the big toe towards the inside edge of the foot whereas the reflex area for the ribs goes right across the whole of the foot at the level of the metatarsals (from the base of the toes to just above the waist line), just as the ribs go from one side of the body to another.

APPLICATION OF TECHNIQUES TO THE BODY

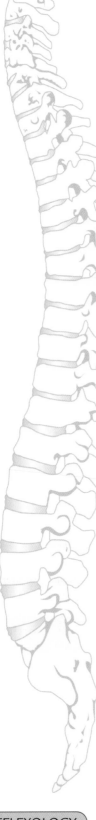

Why work it?
Working these reflexes helps relax the chest area and can be useful for breathing problems.

Reflex for the sacroiliac joint
Where is it?
The spine joins the pelvis at the sacroiliac joint. Its reflex area is very tiny. On the top of the foot, on the outside just below the ankle bone there is a slope as the skin flattens out to form the foot. This is the reflex area for the sacroiliac joint. To check that you have the right spot imagine a straight line from the centre of the base of the fourth toe to the ankle. Where the line reaches the ankle is the reflex.
Why work it?
Working this reflex helps any hip, pelvis or lower back problems. It can also, by association, help the legs.

Reflex for the hip
Where is it?
The heel corresponds to the lower body in reflexology. The hip reflex is thus just before it, on the outside edge of the foot.
Why work it?
Working the hip reflex directly helps problems with the hip joint, pelvis and the lower back but can also benefit the leg.

Reflex for the knee
Where is it?
The knee reflex is just above the hip reflex. It is on the outside edge of the foot, at the level of the arch/waistline.
Why work it?
Working the knee reflex benefits the knee joint, easing pain and stiffness but it can also relieve associated problems such as arthritis, torn ligaments or damaged cartilage.

General summary

Working any of the skeletal reflexes will benefit other parts of the system. However, working these reflexes is especially useful for any of the generalised inflammatory conditions of the joints (any type of rheumatism or arthritis), osteoporosis, sprained ligaments, fractures, slipped discs and general back pain. Furthermore, since the bones provide attachment for the muscles, any work on the skeletal reflexes will also help problems with muscles and their attachments (ligaments and tendons).

Skeletal

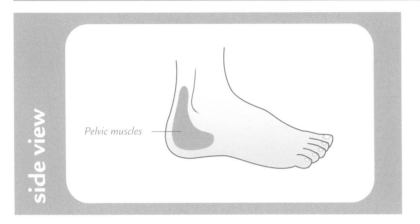

side view

Pelvic muscles

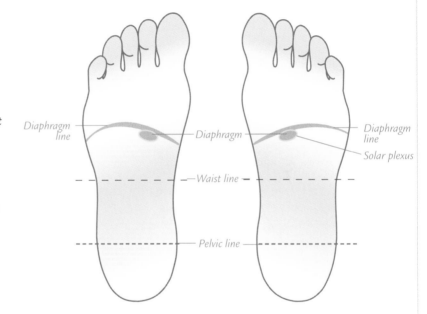

Diaphragm line — Diaphragm — Diaphragm line — Solar plexus

— Waist line —

— Pelvic line —

There are few specific muscular reflexes. The diaphragm is the most important one. As explained above, working the reflexes of the skeletal system (especially the spine) will benefit the muscles, but the nervous system reflexes are also very important since the nerves tell the muscles what to do. In addition, the reflex for the adrenal glands should also be worked in any treatment of the muscular system since the hormones secreted by these glands control muscular tone.

Reflex for the diaphragm

Where is it?

The reflex for the diaphragm is right below the diaphragm line, just on the lower edge of the ball of the foot. The main reflex is almost directly below the second toe but the whole diaphragm line across the foot is associated with it.

Why work it?

The diaphragm reflex is important for relaxing the whole body because working it helps respiratory problems. It is also associated with all stress and stress-related disorders because slowing down breathing by releasing tension in this large muscle will reduce stress.

Reflex for the pelvic muscles

Where is it?

The pelvic area reflex is on the outside of the foot, below the ankle, extending back almost to the heel, behind the ankle bone and down to the sole.

Why work it?

The muscles of the pelvis connect to the hip joint, and leg bones, as well as to the iliac crest which itself joins the spine. Working this reflex will help hip and leg problems, stiffness or misalignment of the pelvis (which themselves affect the legs and lower back) and also lower back problems.

General summary

The muscular system benefits from working any of these three reflexes but also any of the skeletal reflexes to which it connects as well as the nervous system.

THE CIRCULATORY (VASCULAR) SYSTEM

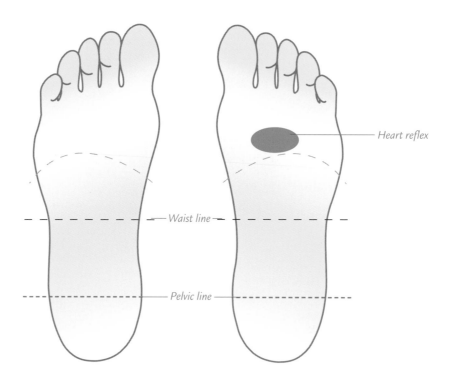

Heart reflex

Waist line

Pelvic line

The circulatory system is the body's fuel and transport system which is driven by the heart, its engine. Working the muscular and nervous reflexes will benefit the circulatory system because a more efficient nervous system will communicate with the heart and blood vessels more quickly and improved muscle function will pump blood faster, thus improving the function of all the cells in the body.

NB It should be remembered that anyone with a serious heart or circulatory condition should check with their GP before having a reflexology treatment.

Reflexes for the blood vessels

Since blood vessels supply the whole body, any circulatory problems in a particular area will be helped by working the general reflex for that area (e.g. working the head reflex will improve blood circulation in the head).

Reflex for the heart
Where is it?
The heart reflex is one of the reflexes which is represented in only one foot, the left. It is just above the diaphragm line, directly below, and extending the width of, the second and third toes.
Why work it?
Working this reflex benefits the overall circulation, helps blood pressure problems and any heart conditions.

General summary

Working the circulatory reflexes benefits the whole body, just as working related systems (muscular, nervous and respiratory) will benefit the circulation.

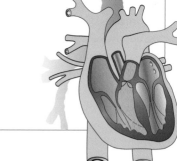

THE LYMPHATIC SYSTEM

The lymphatic system is a secondary circulation that supports the blood circulation, makes antibodies and detoxifies tissue fluid of infections and bacteria.

Reflexes for the lymphatic system and ducts

The lymphatic system is dotted all over the body and particular lymph nodes and areas of circulation can be worked by working that section of the sole or palm (e.g. the lymph nodes in the arm will benefit from working the arm reflex).Lymphatic tissue is also found in the body in places such as the thymus, Peyer's patches, tonsils and appendix. By working over these reflex areas, usually when working other systems, indirect benefits will be gained by the lymphatic system. However, there is also a reflex area for the whole system and for the lymphatic ducts. The reflex for the whole system is a narrow area around the front of the ankle at the point where the leg becomes the top of the foot. The area extends from under the ankle bone on one side to under the ankle bone on the other. The reflex areas for the lymphatic ducts are found on the top of the feet between the metatarsal bones.

Why work them?
Working the lymphatic area benefits the whole of the system, improving the efficiency of its functions: fighting infection, producing antibodies, removing excess fluid from tissues and cells throughout the body.

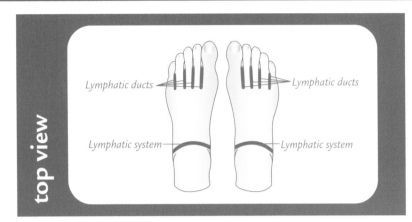

top view

Lymphatic ducts — Lymphatic ducts
Lymphatic system — Lymphatic system

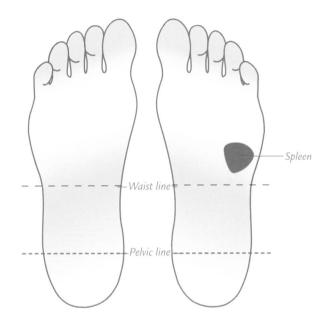

Spleen

Waist line

Pelvic line

Reflex for the spleen
Where is it?
The spleen reflex is on the lower right-hand side of the left sole, just above the waistline, and below the diaphragm line below the join of the fourth and fifth toe.

Why work it?
The spleen makes new lymphocytes and destroys old blood cells. It helps fight infection but is not essential to the body's functions. Working this reflex is useful for treating infections and for stimulating an efficient circulation.

General summary
Working the lymphatic system benefits the whole body, encouraging better fluid drainage from cells and tissues throughout the body and boosting the immune system.

THE NERVOUS SYSTEM

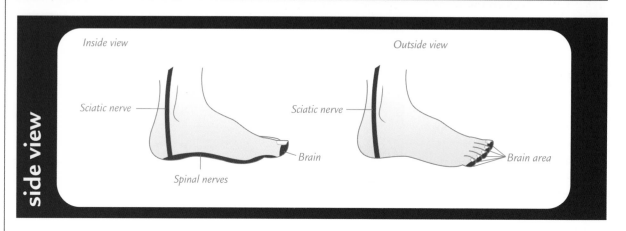

side view

Inside view

Sciatic nerve

Spinal nerves

Brain

Outside view

Sciatic nerve

Brain area

Probably the most important system for reflexology since it has been estimated that there are approximately 7000 nerve endings in the feet, making them particularly sensitive and helpful for accessing the whole body. We have already discussed the spine which is one of the major parts of the central nervous system: the other main component is the brain.

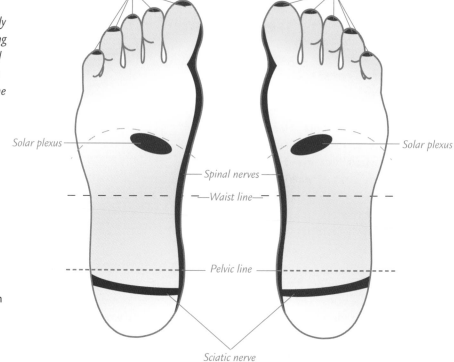

Brain area

Brain area

Solar plexus

Solar plexus

Spinal nerves

Waist line

Pelvic line

Sciatic nerve

Reflexes for the brain
Where are they?
The reflex areas for the brain are in the tips of the big toes. The other toes also help with the work of these reflexes.

Why work them?
Working the brain reflex will affect the whole nervous system, which is controlled by the brain, as well as chronic conditions such as Alzheimer's or Parkinson's. Head-aches, nervous tension and other stress-related problems will all benefit from working these areas.

Reflexes for the sciatic nerve
The sciatic nerve is the largest nerve in the body.
Where are they?
The sciatic nerve reflex areas are narrow, curved bands across the middle of the heels on the bottom

of the feet which then continue up around the ankle bone and the back of the calf.

Why work them?
This nerve connects the legs to the spinal cord and thus any problems with this nerve may

cause discomfort in the lower back and legs. Sciatica, for example, is a condition caused by inflammation of this nerve. Working this area will ease any discomfort or inflammation of the nerve and improve nervous functions in the lower back and limbs.

Reflex for the solar plexus

Like the diaphragm, this reflex is one of the most important in reflexology, especially for combating stress and enabling relaxation. The solar plexus is a bundle of nerves which sits just in front of the diaphragm.

Where is it?

The solar plexus reflex is on the centre of the diaphragm line, overlapping with the diaphragm reflex.

Why work it?

Working the solar plexus induces deep relaxation throughout the body because this bundle of nerves connects to the abdomen, the physical centre of the body, where many stress-related disorders manifest themselves (dyspepsia, IBS, ulcers, constipation, diarrhoea). (See Chapter 4 for more details on deep breathing techniques using the solar plexus reflex.)

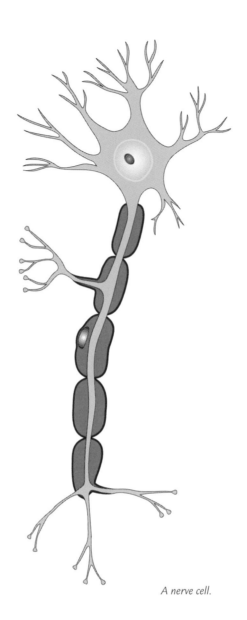

A nerve cell.

General summary

One of reflexology's main benefits is relaxation and working the nervous system is very important for inducing relaxation and thus slowing the body reactions to stress signals. It also improves the efficiency of the body's voluntary functions, by improving the speed and function of the communication network.

Nervous

● THE ENDOCRINE SYSTEM

The endocrine system is a chemical communication network which uses hormones to send messages to the body, telling it how to grow and function. It thus helps maintain homeostasis (a stable, physiological state). Many of the glands that produce these hormones are very small and the corresponding reflex areas on the feet are also small.

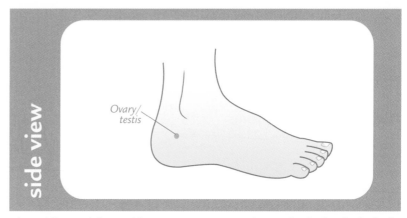

side view

Ovary/ testis

Reflex for the thymus gland

The thymus gland secretes hormones but also produces T lymphocytes, making it part of the lymphatic system as well. It is active before puberty but shrinks in adulthood, thus making it a useful reflex to work on children.

Where is it?

This reflex is on the inside edge of the sole of the foot, just below the big toe and extending down a short distance over the ball of the foot.

Why work it?

The thymus gland helps the correct functioning of the immune system so it should be worked whenever there is a malfunction, generalised infection or simply to boost immunity.

Reflex for the thyroid gland

The thyroid gland is very important because the hormones it secretes control the metabolism and growth. It is in the front of the throat.

Where is it?

The thyroid gland reflex is on the sole of the foot on the 'neck' of the big toe, i.e. the point where the toe joins the foot.

Why work it?

Working the thyroid gland will help the functioning of the metabolism, balancing it and

thus aiding weight problems. It will also help to bring it back into equilibrium, in the case of under or over-activity and their various symptoms (e.g. underactivity causes myxoedema in adults, or cretinism in children and over-activity can cause thyrotoxicosis).

Reflex for the parathyroid glands

The parathyroid glands are located behind the thyroid gland. They secrete parathormone which maintains calcium levels in plasma.

Where is it?

The parathyroid glands reflex is in the same place as the thyroid reflex: on the sole of the foot on the 'neck' of the big toe, i.e. the point where the toe joins the foot.

Why work them?

Working the parathyroid glands reflex helps any calcium deficiency/problems and linked conditions, e.g. muscle spasm: tetany, kidney stones, osteoporosis.

Reflexes for the adrenal glands

These glands are split into two parts, the cortex and the medulla. The cortex secretes hormones that

control growth, the level of salts in the body and sexual development. The medulla secretes adrenaline and noradrenaline, known as the stress hormones. They prepare the body for 'fight or flight' and thus affect the body systems in order to cope with any possible danger (thus increasing the heart rate and constricting the blood vessels to increase pressure). The physical effects of stress begin with very simple manifestations of adrenaline's arrival in the body: sweaty palms, an awareness of the heart beating faster, a 'churning' stomach.

Where are they?

The reflexes for the adrenal glands are on the soles of both feet, in a similar position to that of the actual glands in the body. They are slightly above the waistline, just above the top of the kidney reflex, below the gap between the big and second toe.

Why work them?

Working the adrenal reflexes helps imbalances in the hormonal system. They are also important for treating any stress and stress-related disorders and any inflammatory conditions.

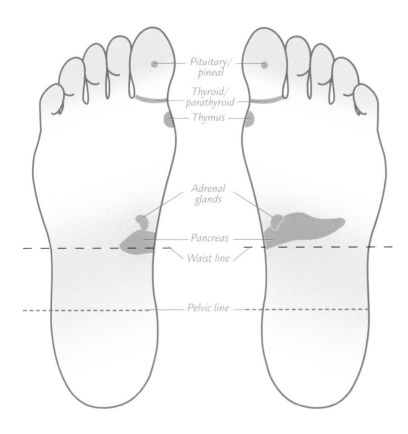

Pituitary/
pineal

Thyroid/
parathyroid

Thymus

Adrenal
glands

Pancreas

Waist line

Pelvic line

disorder (known as S.A.D.) are often cited as symptoms of not enough melatonin, which is produced in response to sunlight.

Where is it?
The pineal gland is in the centre of the brain and similarly the pineal reflex area is in the centre of the part of the foot which represents the brain, the big toe, in practically the same place as the pituitary reflex. Working the pineal will benefit the pituitary and vice versa.

Why work it?
Working the pineal will benefit the body's overall rhythms and encourage efficient melatonin production.

Reflex for the pancreas
Where is it?
Like the organ it represents, the pancreas reflex extends across the 'body', i.e. both feet. On the right foot, the reflex is at the level of the waist line, extending from the inside edge to the join of big and second toe. On the left foot, the reflex extends from the inside edge of the waist line across to the fourth toe. It overlaps with the stomach and kidney reflex.

Why work it?
The pancreas is very important because it produces insulin which regulates blood sugar levels. Imbalances in insulin are very dangerous, causing diabetes and other blood sugar-related conditions. Working this reflex will help the pancreas function and be useful for conditions such as diabetes or problems with digestion.

Reflex for the pituitary gland
The pituitary gland is especially important because it controls both the thyroid gland and the adrenal cortex. It also secretes human growth hormone which regulates height and growth, sex organ hormones which control sexual development and the gonads (ovaries and testes), melanocyte-stimulating hormone which stimulates melanin production and finally an antidiuretic hormone which regulates the functions of the kidneys. It is located at the base of the brain and has three hormone-secreting lobes.

Where is it?
The pituitary gland reflex is right in the centre of the fleshy pad of the big toe.

Why work it?
Working the pituitary benefits hormonal functioning and balance throughout the body.

Reflex for the pineal gland
The pineal gland, or pineal body as it is sometimes called, secretes melatonin which controls the body's natural rhythms: depression and seasonal affective

General summary
Working the endocrine system benefits the whole body, improving the production of hormones and their subsequent functions.

THE REPRODUCTIVE SYSTEM

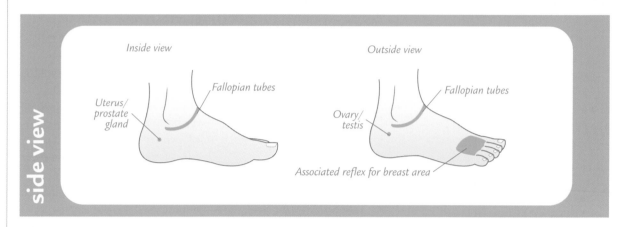

side view

Inside view

*Uterus/
prostate
gland*

Fallopian tubes

Outside view

Fallopian tubes

*Ovary/
testis*

Associated reflex for breast area

*This system enables
humans to reproduce.*

Reflex for the uterus
Where is it?
The reflex for the uterus is on the inside of the foot on the side, on a mid-point of an imaginary diagonal between the ankle bone and the back of the heel.
Why work it?
This reflex should be worked for any menstrual or menopausal problems. However, reflexology is not usually advised during a heavy period.

Reflex for the ovary
Where is it?
The reflex area for the ovary is in the same place as the uterus reflex but on the outside of the foot: on the midpoint of a diagonal from the ankle bone to the back of the heel.
Why work it?
This reflex is important for any menstrual or menopausal problems and also infertility.

Reflex for the Fallopian tubes
Where is it?
The reflex for the Fallopian tubes

is in the same place as the reflex for both the lymphatic system and the groin. This is a narrow area around the front of the ankle at the point where the leg becomes the top of the foot. The area extends right across from under the ankle bone on one side to under the ankle bone on the other.
Why work it?
This reflex is important for any

menstrual or menopausal problems and also infertility.

Reflexes for the breasts
Where are they?
There is a reflex for the left and right breast on the ball of each foot in the same position as the lung reflexes. An associated reflex on the top of the foot is the area below the toes between the

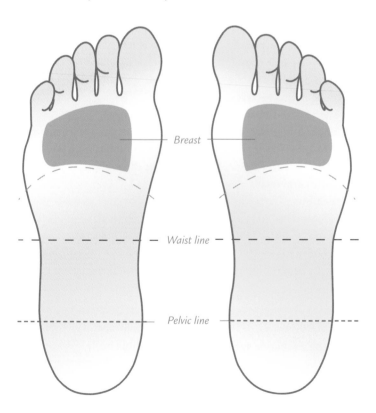

Breast

Waist line

Pelvic line

metatarsals. Since the ball of the foot is quite thick it is sometimes easier to work these reflexes by using the top not the sole of the foot.

Why work them?

Working the breast reflexes is important for any problems with the breasts and is also beneficial for the lymphatic system because there are lots of nodes in and around the breasts.

Reflex for the prostate gland

Where is it?

The reflex for the prostate gland is the same as the uterus reflex: on the inside of the foot on the side, on a mid-point of a diagonal between the ankle bone and the back of the heel.

Why work it?

Working the prostate reflex will be important for the male reproductive system in general but is also useful in specific cases affecting the gland.

Reflexes for the testes

Where are they?

The reflex area for each testis is in the same place as the ovary reflex: on the outside of the foot, on the side, on a midpoint of a diagonal from the ankle bone to the back of the heel.

Why work them?

Working the testes reflexes is important for the male reproductive system in general.

General summary

Working the reproductive system is particularly important for those trying to conceive but also helps prevent infections and menstrual/menopausal problems.

Reproductive

● THE DIGESTIVE SYSTEM

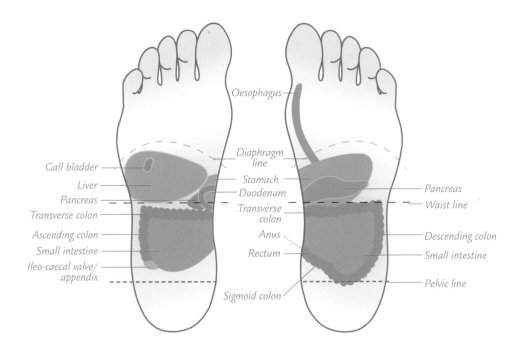

Oesophagus

Gall bladder

Liver

Pancreas

Transverse colon

Ascending colon

Small intestine

Ileo-caecal valve/
appendix

Diaphragm
line

Stomach

Duodenum

Transverse
colon

Anus

Rectum

Sigmoid colon

Pancreas

Waist line

Descending colon

Small intestine

Pelvic line

When we breathe we take in what we need and expel what we don't need. The digestive system works in the same way: we eat and the body takes the nutrients it needs from the food and expels the rest as waste.

Reflex for the oesophagus

This is the tube that takes food from the mouth to the stomach.

Where is it?

The oesophagus reflex is on the sole of the left foot. It descends from the base of the big toe on the inside edge of the foot to just above the diaphragm.

Why work it?

To encourage better digestion.

Reflex for the stomach

Where is it?

The stomach reflex is directly below the diaphragm line and above the waist line on both feet, though it extends from the inside

of the foot to the width of the third toe on the left foot and only across from the inside of the foot to the width of the big toe on the right foot.

Why work it?

To encourage better digestion and for stomach disorders.

Reflexes for the small intestine

Where are they?

The small intestine reflexes are directly below the waist line, in the arches. The reflex extends across from the inside edge of the feet almost to the outside.

Why work them?

To encourage better digestion.

Reflex for the duodenum

The duodenum is the first part of the small intestine.

Where is it?

The duodenal reflex is on the sole

of the right foot, on the inside edge. It is a narrow C-shape that starts just above the waist line and ends just below it at the level of the small intestine reflex.

Why work it?

To encourage better digestion.

Reflex for the ileo-caecal valve and appendix

The link between the small and large intestine is the ileo-caecal valve. The appendix is a small organ that connects to the beginning of the large intestine, close to the ileo-caecal valve. It contains a lot of lymphatic tissue and is therefore useful in infections but it often becomes infected itself and is removed.

Where is it?

The reflex for both the valve and the appendix is on the sole of the right foot to the left of the small intestine reflex and below the start of the large intestine reflex.

Why work it?

To help balance the lymphatic system (appendix) and bowel function.

Reflexes for the large intestine

Where are they?

The large intestine has several parts: the caecum, colon (ascending, transverse and descending), the rectum and anus. Again the reflex on the soles of the feet reflects the position and shape of the organs. Thus the whole reflex is below the waist line and travels across both feet. The ascending colon reflex is on the sole of the right foot, a narrow line to the left of the small intestine reflex travelling up to the waist line. The transverse colon reflex then travels across the extent of the right sole from the ascending colon to the inside edge of the foot, directly below the waist line. In the middle of the sole of the left foot, again at the waist line, the transverse colon reflex continues across (extending across zones one to four) almost to the outside edge of the foot to between zones four and five where the descending colon reflex starts. This runs down the outside of the left sole and angles in across the arch to the beginning of the heel, at the level of the pelvic line and sciatic nerve reflex. It then curves back up and across to the inside edge of the foot: this part of the reflex is the sigmoid colon (the curved part of the colon which joins the rectum). The reflex for the rectum and anus is postioned at the end of the sigmoid colon, where it reaches the inside of the foot and the spine reflex.

Why work them?

To improve bowel function, prevent constipation and help the efficiency of the digestive system.

The accessory organs

The accessory organs to digestion, the liver, pancreas and gall bladder, are all associated with the digestive process. Food does not pass through them but they produce or store substances that help with digestion.

Reflex for the liver

Where is it?

The reflex for the liver is on the right foot. It extends across the whole sole and is situated just below the diaphragm line and just above the waist line.

Why work it?

The liver is the largest and one of the most important glands in the body. It has many functions including removing toxins from the blood, storing vital substances such as vitamins, iron and glycogen and producing heat, bile and vitamin A. Working this reflex will help improve the efficiency of all liver functions.

Reflex for the gall bladder

The gall bladder is a small sac-like organ attached to the liver.

Where is it?

The reflexes for the gall bladder and liver, like the organs of the alimentary canal, are connected. The gall bladder reflex is a small area, in the same place as the liver reflex, on the sole of the right foot. It is towards the outside edge of the liver reflex, in the centre of the area above the waist line and below the diaphragm line, directly below the fourth toe.

Why work it?

The gall bladder stores bile that the liver has produced and is not using. Bile is used to emulsify fats so working the gall bladder will improve the efficiency of fat digestion.

Reflex for the pancreas

Where is it?

Like the organ it represents, the pancreas reflex extends across the 'body' i.e. both feet. On the right foot, the reflex is at the level of the waistline, extending from the inside edge to the join of big and second toe. On the left foot, the reflex extends from the inside edge of the waist line across to the fourth toe. It overlaps with the stomach and kidney reflex.

Why work it?

The pancreas is very important because it produces insulin which regulates blood sugar levels. Imbalances in insulin are very dangerous, causing diabetes and other blood sugar-related conditions. Working this reflex will help the pancreas function and be useful for conditions such as diabetes or problems associated with digestion.

General summary

Without nutrients we would not survive so it is essential that the food we eat is converted as quickly as possible so that the body can use it. Efficient digestion enables the body to function properly and prevents fatigue, constipation and stomach problems. Working the digestive reflexes encourages the digestive system to work correctly.

APPLICATION OF TECHNIQUES TO THE BODY

THE RESPIRATORY SYSTEM

The respiratory system is fundamental to life. It is the body's breathing apparatus and humans cannot survive without air for more than a couple of minutes. Every single cell of the body breathes 'in' and 'out' millions of times during one day.

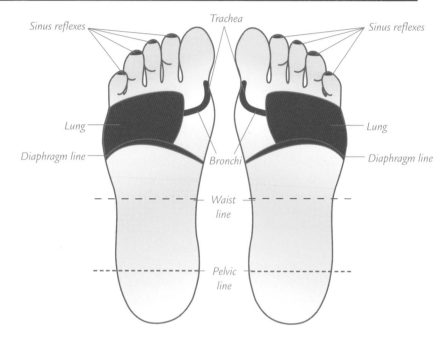

Reflex for the nose

The nose permits the passage of air into the body. It is lined with minute hairs, cilia, that pick up debris and filter the air that is breathed in. Mucus lining the nasal cavities traps the particles which are then expelled through sneezing or by blowing the nose. Olfactory receptor cells (chemoreceptors) within the tissues lining the roof of the nasal cavity detect odours. Nerves fibres pass through to the olfactory bulb and then the olfactory tract sending impulses back to the olfactory nerves in the brain. The sense of smell is linked to taste and appetite. The loss of the sense of smell is known as anosmia; it is normally caused by inflammation of the nasal tissues. Changes to the sense of taste, dysgeusia, or the loss of taste, ageusia, may often link to the loss of smell.
Where are they?
The reflex areas for the nose are found on the front of the big toe, below the nail, towards the midline.
Why work them?
Working these reflexes will help with nasal congestion, colds and conditions such as hay fever or allergies, when irritation may be present.

Reflexes for the lungs, trachea and bronchi

The trachea is the tube through which air passes from the nose to the bronchi and the bronchi take air into the lungs. In exhalation the process is reversed (lungs, bronchi, trachea). The lungs are two spongy organs where gaseous exchange takes place (the passage of oxygen to the body and carbon dioxide from the body).
Where are they?
The reflexes for the lungs extend across the balls of both feet from the inside to outside edge, under the toes and above the diaphragm line. Their position on the map of the feet is very similar to their position in the body. The trachea and bronchi reflexes, like the actual passages, lead down from the head reflex and across to the lung.
Why work them?
Working these reflexes will help the whole respiratory system function more efficiently.

Reflexes for the sinuses

The sinuses are hollow spaces inside the bones around the nose.
Where are they?
The reflex areas for the sinuses are in the tip of the toes (but not in the big toe).
Why work them?
Working these reflexes will encourage the clearing out of infection or congestion from the sinuses and helps with colds, flu, hay fever and headaches.

General summary

Working the respiratory system reflexes will help the whole body, ensuring that oxygen gets into cells and carbon dioxide is taken out of them. Working the circulatory, nervous and muscular systems will also benefit the respiratory system.

THE URINARY SYSTEM

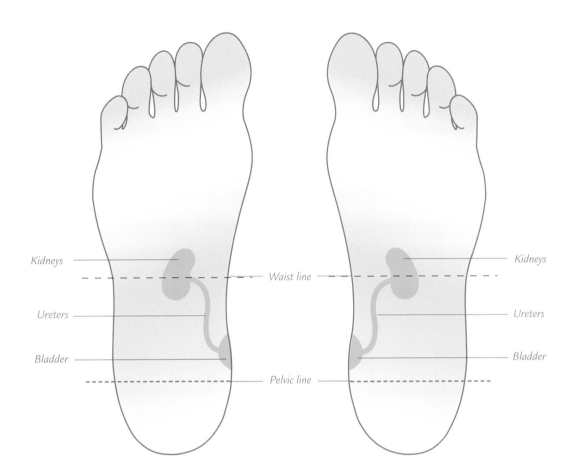

Kidneys — — — — Waist line — — — Kidneys

Ureters — — Ureters

Bladder — — Bladder

Pelvic line

This system is the body's waste disposal and filtration unit.

Reflexes for the kidneys

Where are they?
There is a reflex for each kidney on each sole. It is located in the middle of the sole, at the level of the waist line, almost directly below the second toe.

Why work them?
Working the kidney reflexes benefits the whole excretion process, making it more efficient.

Reflexes for the ureters

Where are they?
The reflexes for the ureter tubes run

from the kidney reflexes at waist line level, out to the inside edge of the soles and the bladder reflex.

Why work them?
Working these reflexes encourages a more efficient removal of urine and the clearing out of infections and kidney stones.

Reflex for the bladder

Where is it?
The bladder reflex is found on both

soles of the feet on the inside edge just above the start of the heels and the sacrum/coccyx reflex.

Why work it?
Working the bladder reflex encourages more efficient functioning of the muscle, including better control in cases of incontinence as well as clearing out of infections.

General summary

Working the urinary system reflexes encourages waste removal and helps prevent infections of, and problems with, the kidney and bladder.

OTHER REFLEXES

Reflex for the skin

Where is it?

The skin is the body's outer layer, protecting it and helping it excrete and absorb substances. The reflex areas are in the same areas of the foot as the part of skin that is being treated. So the skin on the face will benefit by treating the reflex area for the face, the skin on the legs by treating the reflex area for the legs and so on. Many sensory nerve receptors are found within the layers of the skin. Nociceptors, which respond to stimulation causing pain are found in the skin. Free nerve endings also register pain. Mechanoreceptors such as

Merkel's discs, Meissner's corpuscles and Pacinian corpuscles register touch and pressure. Thermoreceptors are sensitive to changes in temperature. Krause's end bulbs and Ruffini corpuscles are found in the skin and are sensitive to cold and heat. Chemoreceptors are found in the tissues lining the mouth and nose and respond to taste and smell.

Why work it?

Working the skin is helpful for any skin condition (such as psoriasis, acne, rashes) and also for a general sense of well-being because the skin is the organ of touch.

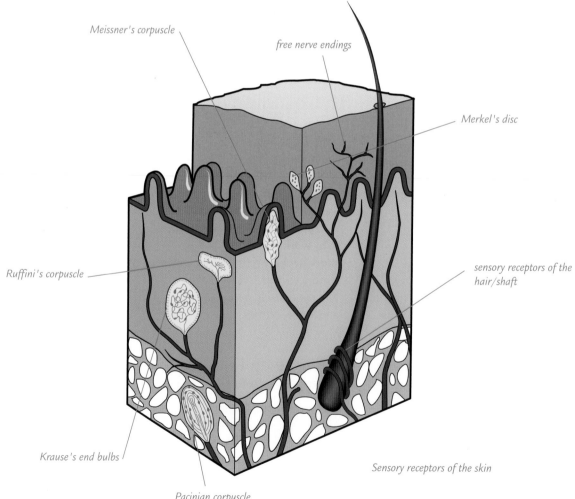

Meissner's corpuscle

free nerve endings

Merkel's disc

Ruffini's corpuscle

sensory receptors of the hair/shaft

Krause's end bulbs

Pacinian corpuscle

Sensory receptors of the skin

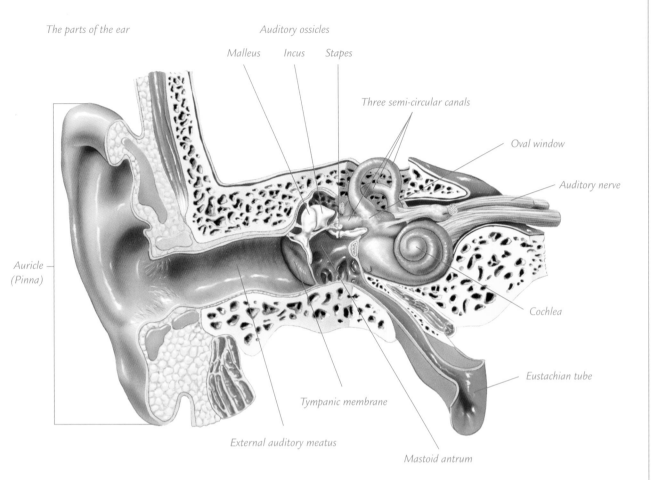

The parts of the ear

Auditory ossicles

Malleus Incus Stapes

Three semi-circular canals

Oval window

Auditory nerve

Auricle
(Pinna)

Cochlea

Eustachian tube

Tympanic membrane

External auditory meatus

Mastoid antrum

The Ears

The ears provide hearing and maintain body balance. The ear structure has three parts - the outer ear, the middle ear and the inner ear.

The outer ear

The outer ear is the visible part of the ear. It protects the inner structures from damage. The External auditory meatus (auditory canal) is lined with ceruminous glands and hairs, which filter out dust and foreign particles. The outer ear is also the passage for sound waves. The tympanic membrane (eardrum) separates the auditory canal from the middle ear.

The middle ear

The middle ear is found within a cavity in the temporal bone. It has minute bones known as auditory ossicles that transmit sounds from the tympanic membrane to the inner ear.

The inner ear

The inner ear is responsible for hearing and balance. Within the inner ear structures, the vibrations of sound waves are translated into nerve impulses. Structures within the inner ear, the semicircular canals and vestibule, help to maintain posture and balance.

The Eustachian tube

The Eustachian tube connects the middle ear to the throat. It maintains the atmospheric pressure of air within the ear, enabling the eardrum to vibrate as the sound waves reach it. This is vital for hearing.

Cross-section of nose and olfactory tract.

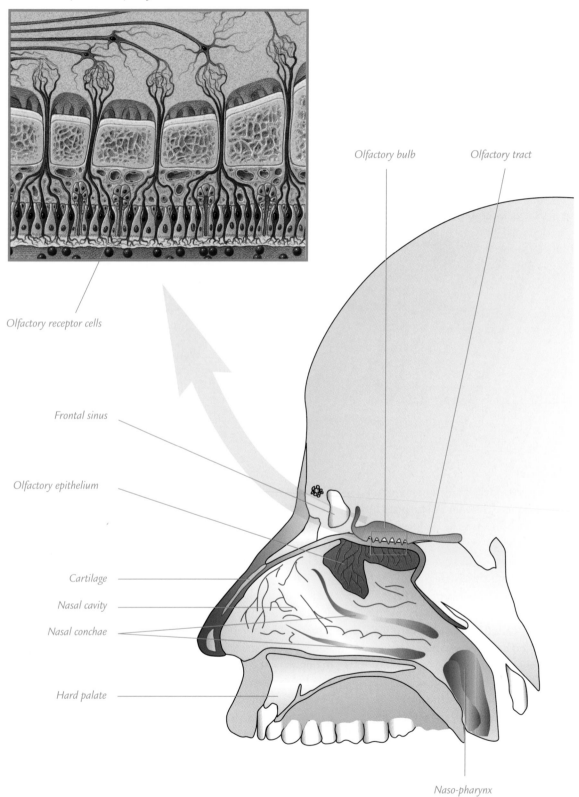

Olfactory receptor cells

Olfactory bulb

Olfactory tract

Frontal sinus

Olfactory epithelium

Cartilage

Nasal cavity

Nasal conchae

Hard palate

Naso-pharynx

The ears are complex, sensitive organs and are susceptible to damage in many ways. Loud noise or trauma many damage the sensitive receptors in the ears, causing hearing loss. Viral or bacterial infections may cause disorders such as otitis media. Problems with the inner ear can cause conditions such as Meniere's disease, tinnitus, vertigo or labrynthitis, which affect the balance and health of the client.

The Eyes

The eyes are the organs of sight. They are positioned separately, but function generally as a pair, assisting in the maintenance of balance.

The eyelids are layers of tissue above and below the front of the eye. They protect the eyes through blinking (20-30 times per minute) and the eyelashes that line the edges of the eyelids filter and trap substances such as dust. Sebaceous and mucus secretions lubricate the eyelids. Lacrimal glands secrete a fluid that keeps the surface of the eye moist and prevents the cornea from drying out. If a foreign body enters the eye, extra fluid is produced to wash away the particle. Parasympathetic stimulation of these glands causes crying, when large amounts of fluid are produced.

The eyes have a fibrous outer layer known as the sclera or white of eye. At the front of the eye this is covered by a thin mucous membrane, the conjunctiva. The conjunctiva also lines the inside of the eyelids and helps prevents damage

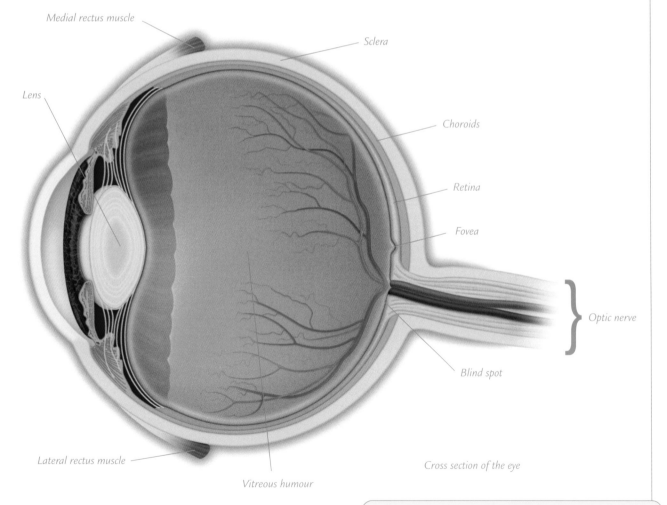

Medial rectus muscle

Sclera

Lens

Choroids

Retina

Fovea

Optic nerve

Blind spot

Lateral rectus muscle

Vitreous humour

Cross section of the eye

APPLICATION OF TECHNIQUES TO THE BODY

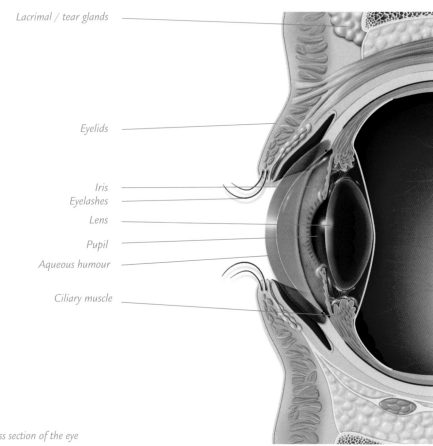

Lacrimal / tear glands

Eyelids

Iris
Eyelashes
Lens
Pupil
Aqueous humour

Ciliary muscle

Cross section of the eye

and drying of the eye through mucus secretions. Light enters the eye through a transparent dome, the cornea, and it is focused onto the retina at the back of the eye. It passes through the cornea, the pupil and the iris. The iris is the coloured disc in the centre of the eye, and it controls the amount of light entering through dilation or contraction of the pupil, which appears as a black dot in the middle. The pupil dilates when the light is low and contracts when the light is bright, permitting or restricting the passage of light through the opening. The lens of the eye sits behind the pupil and refracts (bends) light reflected by objects. The ciliary muscles control the thickness of the lens, refracting light and allowing the eyes to focus. The lens becomes thicker to focus on objects nearby and thinner to focus on objects in the distance. The retina forms the inner

layer of the eye wall. It contains light sensitive cells (photoreceptors). Near the centre of the retina is the macula, which is highly sensitive and contains millions of photoreceptors called rods and cones. The photoreceptors permit the conversion of light rays into nerve impulses. In the centre of the retina is a small dimple, the fovea, which provides sharpest vision and is the location of most colour perception At the nasal side of the macula, the nerve fibres gather to form the optic nerve, one of the cranial nerves. This nerve leaves the eye through an area known as the blind spot. The blind spot has no light sensitive cells. The eyeball is divided into two sections, each one filled with fluid. These fluids maintain the internal pressure and shape of the eyeball. Aqueous humour fills the space between the cornea and the lens, providing nourishment to the tissues.

Vitreous humour fills the eye from the rear of the lens to the retina. It is a jellylike fluid that contains water and salts.

Sight impairment or loss may occur through natural degeneration of the eye structures, wear and tear or trauma. Conditions such as cataracts, corneal ulcers and glaucoma are progressive and require medical intervention to prevent loss of sight.

Common conditions that are uncomfortable but that do not threaten the sight such as blepharitis and conjunctivitis can occur due to viral or bacterial infection. Contact lens wearers or allergy sufferers may experience sensitive eyes and need to ensure that good standards of hygiene are maintained if touching the eye area to prevent irritation.

The tongue and the sense of taste

The tongue is a muscular organ, covered with a membrane. It is held in place by attachments to the mandible (lower jaw) and the hyoid bone. Tiny projections known as papillae cover the top, increasing its surface area and producing a rough texture. Sensory nerve endings in the papillae form what we commonly know as taste buds.

Functions: the tongue has three digestive functions — taste, chewing and swallowing:

taste: the tongue is covered with thousands of taste buds which are sensitive to salt, sweet, sour and bitter chemicals in food and drink. They help us enjoy what we eat and drink and act as the first line of defence, warning us when food, drink or foreign matter are off or inedible.

chewing: the tongue aids chewing by moving food around the mouth, pushing it between the teeth and covering it with saliva, which contains enzymes that start the digestive process. The food is turned into a partially digested mass known as a bolus.

swallowing: when the food is ready to travel to the stomach, the tongue pushes it to the back of the mouth.

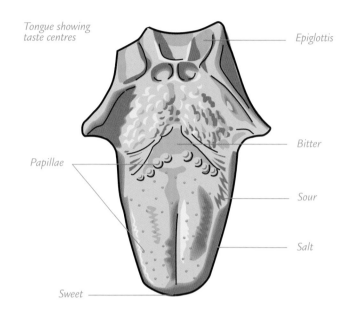

Tongue showing taste centres

Epiglottis

Papillae

Bitter

Sour

Salt

Sweet

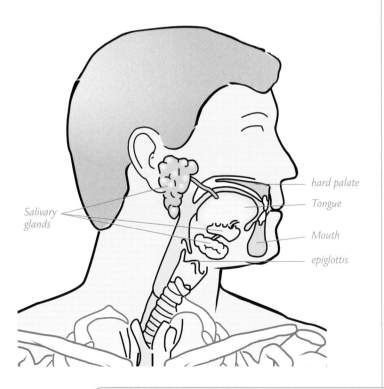

Salivary glands

hard palate

Tongue

Mouth

epiglottis

What is saliva?

Saliva is a liquid secreted by three pairs of salivary glands: the parotid gland (situated below the ear), the submandibular gland and the sublingual gland (both situated below the tongue). It contains water, mucus and the enzyme salivary amylase.

Saliva has three functions:

• to lubricate the food with mucus, making it easier to swallow

• to start digestion: it contains the enzyme salivary amylase, which acts on cooked starch turning it into shorter polysaccharides

• to keep the mouth and teeth clean.

Taste function may be lost or impaired by medication, vitamin deficiency, as a symptom of specific diseases, or simply because of a dry mouth.

Reflexes for the eyes, ears and Eustachian tube

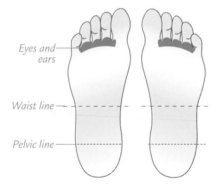

Where are they?

The reflexes for the eyes and ears are narrow strips on both feet, situated at the base of the second, third and fourth toes, above the lung reflexes. The reflex for the Eustachian tube is found on the sole of the foot just below the skin between the third and fourth toes.

Why work them?

Working the eyes, ears and Eustachian tube reflexes benefits their overall function, as well as being useful for specific conditions such as infections,

hearing and balance problems and glaucoma.

Reflex for the throat

Where is it?

The throat reflex is in the same place as the reflexes for the neck and thyroid: a narrow strip around the base of each big toe.

Why work it?

Working the throat reflex is helpful for any throat infections, will encourage the healing response of the tonsils, thyroid glands and ease any stiffness in the neck and throat.

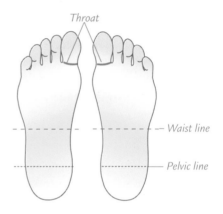

Reflex for the face

Where is it?

The reflex area for the face is on the top of the big toe, around the base of the nail and down to the base of the toe.

Why work it?

Working the face reflex affects the whole face, lips, mouth, teeth and nose and can be beneficial for pains such as toothache, skin conditions and nasal problems.

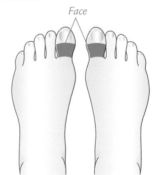

6 Treating specific conditions

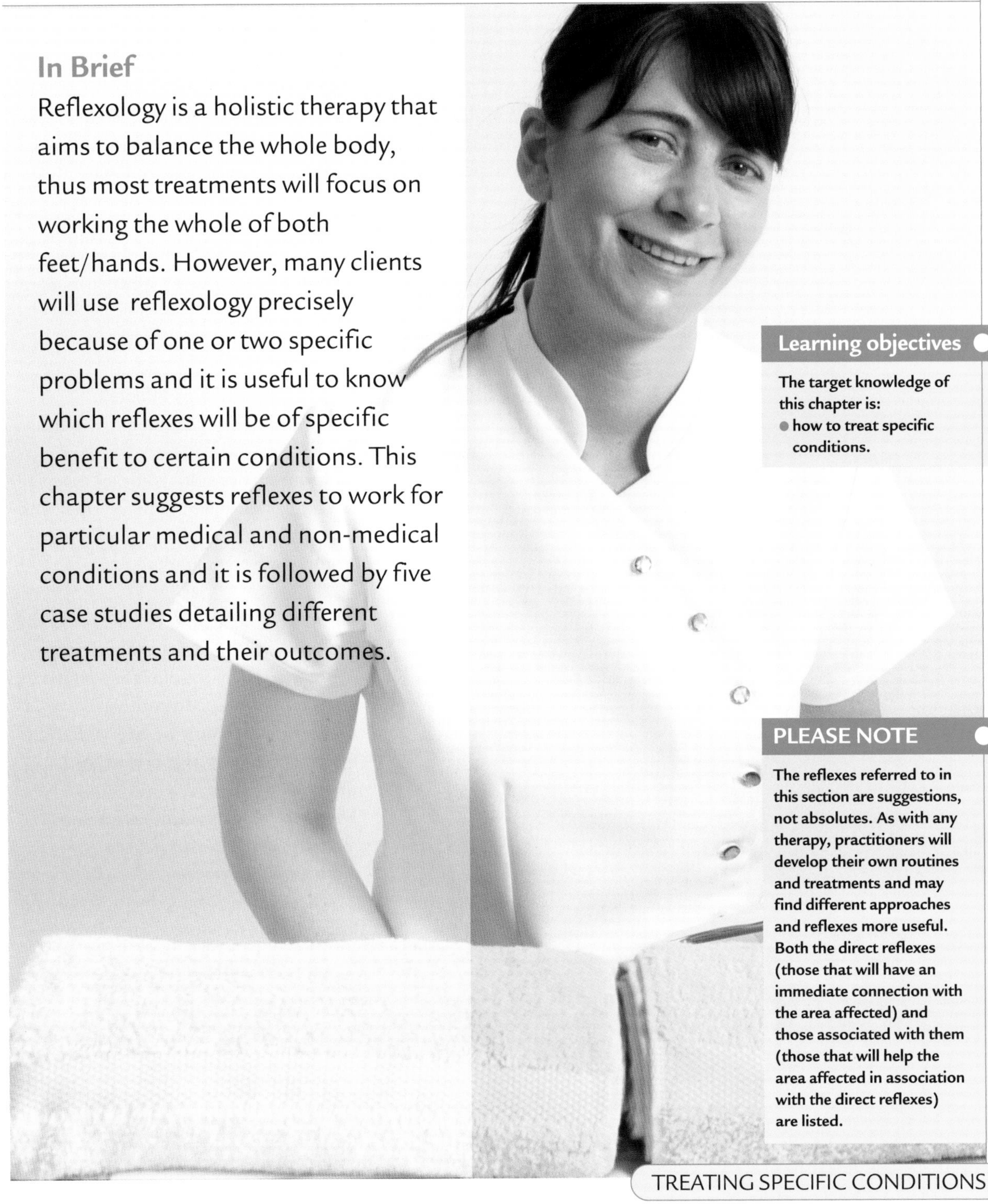

In Brief

Reflexology is a holistic therapy that aims to balance the whole body, thus most treatments will focus on working the whole of both feet/hands. However, many clients will use reflexology precisely because of one or two specific problems and it is useful to know which reflexes will be of specific benefit to certain conditions. This chapter suggests reflexes to work for particular medical and non-medical conditions and it is followed by five case studies detailing different treatments and their outcomes.

Learning objectives

The target knowledge of this chapter is:
● how to treat specific conditions.

PLEASE NOTE

The reflexes referred to in this section are suggestions, not absolutes. As with any therapy, practitioners will develop their own routines and treatments and may find different approaches and reflexes more useful. Both the direct reflexes (those that will have an immediate connection with the area affected) and those associated with them (those that will help the area affected in association with the direct reflexes) are listed.

THE SKIN

Acne

Acne affects both men and women. Poor diet, lack of fluids particularly water, and constipation should be taken into consideration in any treatment for skin problems. There are two main types of acne: *acne vulgaris* and *acne rosacea*.

Acne vulgaris

Cause: usually caused by hormonal imbalances which increase sebum production and thus blocked pores and infection

Effect: the skin becomes shiny and sallow, with pustules and blackheads.

Acne rosacea

Cause: often also caused by hormones, especially at menopause

Effect: it gives the skin a red, flushed appearance and can be aggravated by spicy food, changes in temperature and alcohol

Direct: reflex for area affected (thus the face for acne on the face)

Associated: pituitary, thyroid, parathyroids, adrenals, ovaries, testes, liver, gall bladder, kidneys, large intestine, small intestine, stomach, diaphragm, solar plexus.

Eczema

Cause: allergies, stress, adverse reaction to drugs or chemicals

Effect: scaly patches and itching; not contagious.

Dermatitis

Cause: allergies, stress, adverse reaction to drugs or chemicals

Effect: inflammation, blisters and swelling

Direct: reflex for area affected (thus the arm for eczema or dermatitis on the arm)

Associated: hormonal reflexes especially adrenal glands, liver, kidneys, small and large intestine, diaphragm, solar plexus, lymphatic system, immune system.

Psoriasis

This non-contagious skin condition is characterised by red patches covered in silvery scales that constantly flake off. It may affect the whole body or specific areas. The causes of psoriasis are unknown.

Direct: reflex for area affected (thus the face for psoriasis on the face)

Associated: hormonal reflexes especially adrenal glands, liver, kidneys, small and large intestine, diaphragm, solar plexus.

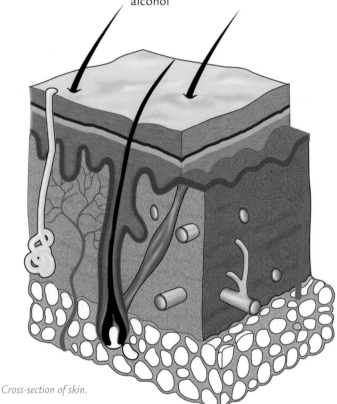

Cross-section of skin.

Skin

THE SKELETAL SYSTEM

A general treatment will benefit the whole skeletal system but a particular part of the body can be treated by focusing on the reflexes for that area. Reflexology can be used to treat slipped discs, stiffness and lower back pain and conditions that affect the joints, such as arthritis and rheumatism.

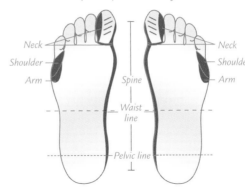

Reflexes of the skeletal system.

Neck — Neck
Shoulder — Shoulder
Arm — Arm
Spine
Waist line
Pelvic line

Neck

Direct: neck, cervical spine
Associated: arm, solar plexus.

Shoulder

Direct: shoulder and shoulder girdle
Associated: neck, cervical spine, solar plexus, adrenal glands.

Elbow

Direct: elbow
Associated: shoulder, arm, neck, adrenal glands (in cases of inflammation).

Lower back

Direct: spine (lumbar, sacral, coccyx)
Associated: sacroiliac joint, pelvic muscles, sciatic nerve, solar plexus, adrenal glands.

Hip

Direct: hip
Associated: spine (lumbar, sacral, coccyx), pelvic muscles, sciatic nerve, solar plexus, adrenal glands.

Fractures and sprains

An overall treatment will encourage the healing process required for these conditions.

Arthritis

Arthritis is an inflammation of the joints and it exists in many different forms: mono-articular arthritis affects one joint; poly-articular affects several; rheumatoid arthritis is a type of poly-arthritis; osteo-arthritis is a chronic arthritis that affects the cartilage in the joints; gout is a painful build-up of uric acid in the joint of the big toe making it swollen and painful.

Direct: for all cases of arthritis, treat the reflexes of those joints and areas affected by pain and inflammation. Since gout affects the big toe it is helpful to treat the thumb rather than the big toe.

Associated: solar plexus, kidneys, adrenal glands (for inflammation), parathyroids. Often treating the whole hormonal system, especially in young people, can have a balancing and unblocking effect on the symptoms.

The spine.

Skeletal

THE MUSCULAR SYSTEM

There are very few specific muscular reflexes except for the diaphragm reflex. Thus the muscular system benefits from a general reflexology treatment. When treating a specific muscular problem, such as a strain, sprain or rupture, treatment will include particular focus on the area affected, e.g. a sprain in a neck muscle will be treated by working the neck reflex, a rupture in a knee ligament will be treated by working the knee reflex.

Cross-section of a muscle

Fibrositis and other muscular conditions

Direct: the reflexes for the muscles in the area affected – thus the back reflex for muscle problems in the back and so on.
Associated: skeletal, circulatory, nervous and endocrine reflexes in the area affected.

THE CIRCULATORY SYSTEM

Any heart conditions must be treated very carefully to avoid overstimulating the heart. As with all medical problems, a GP's advice should be sought on whether a client is able to receive treatment. For example, thrombosis (blood clots) and phlebitis (inflammation of a vein) are contraindicated.

Angina
Sudden attacks of pain behind sternum and in left arm, sometimes accompanied by a feeling of suffocation, caused by reduced blood supply to the middle layer (myocardium) of the heart's wall.
Direct: heart
Associated: solar plexus, adrenal glands, shoulder and arm (if necessary).

Arteriosclerosis and atherosclerosis
In both these conditions the artery walls harden, become less elastic and thus blood pressure increases. Arteriosclerosis is degenerative and mainly affects the elderly. Atherosclerosis is caused by a build-up of fats inside the vessels.
Direct: general treatment, with focus on adrenal glands and thyroid. Associated: Liver, gall bladder, lymphatic system.

Varicose veins
This condition often occurs in the legs, and is caused by standing up for long periods, pregnancy and/or is inherited. The valves in the veins of the legs, which enable venous return, no longer work properly and the veins become distended and knobbly. A condition which may be contraindicated for reflexology. Medical advice should be sought.
Direct: heart, reflex area affected
Associated: intestines, liver, adrenal glands.

Hypertension (high blood pressure)
Blood pressure is the force exerted by the blood on the walls of the blood vessels. Pressure that consistently registers above the normal level for a particular age group is considered to be high blood pressure.
Direct: heart
Associated: solar plexus, adrenal glands, kidneys, head, brain.

Haemorrhoids
Dilated veins in the anus and rectum, usually caused by constipation.
Direct: rectum and anus
Associated: large intestine, solar plexus, adrenal glands.

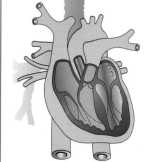
Cross-section of the heart

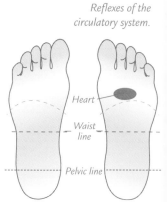
Reflexes of the circulatory system.

Heart
Waist line
Pelvic line

THE LYMPHATIC SYSTEM

Any infection in the body will benefit from working the lymphatic system.

General infections
Direct: lymphatic system
Associated: reflex of area affected.

Fluid retention, swelling
Direct: kidneys, heart
Associated: adrenal glands, lymphatic system.

Throat infections
Direct: throat
Associated: neck, reflex areas to lymph nodes of upper body.

Glandular fever
Caused by the Epstein-Barr virus. Symptoms include fever, enlargement of glands, sore throat, lack of energy.
Direct: a general treatment with focus on lymphatic system.

Leukaemia
An increase in leucocytes in the blood preventing blood forming properly. Symptoms include enlarged spleen and

lymph glands. Medical advice must be sought before treatment.
Direct: lymphatic system, spleen
Associated: all glands.

AIDS (Acquired Immuno-Deficiency Syndrome)
Caused by the HIV virus which reduces immunity. The body is thus not protected from infection and even a cold may be dangerous. Considered fatal but now often controlled by drugs. The virus is spread through sexual intercourse, infected blood, sharing needles and from an infected mother to foetus. The risk to a reflexologist is minimal provided there are no cuts or sores on the skin. Contact surfaces should be sterilised and disposable gloves and towels used.
Direct: general treatment.

Lymphatic ducts *Lymphatic ducts* *Reflexes of the lymphatic system.*

Waist line

Pelvic line

Lymphatic system *Spleen*

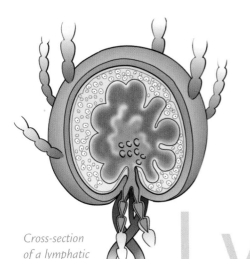

Cross-section of a lymphatic node

Lymphatic

THE NERVOUS SYSTEM

Parkinson's disease
This is a degenerative and progressive disease which affects the basal ganglia of the cerebrum, causing a reduction in dopamine (a neurotransmitter). Symptoms include tremor, muscle stiffness and weakness, and slow voluntary movements. Reflexology can help the symptoms.
Direct: head, brain
Associated: spine, adrenal glands, diaphragm, solar plexus.

Multiple sclerosis
This disease is caused by the loss of the protective myelin sheath from the nerve fibres in the central nervous system. The symptoms include muscular weakness, loss of co-ordination, problems with speech and ataxis (jerky, irregular movements).
Direct: head, brain, spine
Associated: adrenal glands, solar plexus, limbs affected, bladder, eyes, large intestine.

Headaches, migraines
Headaches occur for many reasons and a general treatment may be the most useful approach since stress and tension throughout the body are major contributing factors. Migraines are much more serious headaches, which can cause vomiting and disturbances in vision and usually affect one side of the head. Food allergies can cause attacks as can increased nervous tension.
Direct: head, neck
Associated: face, sinuses, eyes, cervical spine, solar plexus, stomach, small and large intestine, liver, gall bladder, pituitary, thyroid, adrenals, ovaries.

Stroke – cerebral haemorrhage
A cerebral haemorrhage on one side of the brain may cause total or partial paralysis on the opposite side of the body. The effects of a stroke depend on how much of the brain was deprived of its blood and therefore oxygen supply and thus may be simply temporary weakness or complete paralysis on one side of the body. It is important to work the big toe on the opposite side of the body to the affected side (so left big toe for right paralysis and vice versa).
Direct: head, spine, brain, areas affected by stroke
Associated: heart, solar plexus, adrenal glands.

Epilepsy
Two types of epilepsy exist: major and minor. The first causes giddiness and fits and may lead to coma and the second causes blackouts but not fits.
Direct: whole spine
Associated: diaphragm, solar plexus, neck, ileo-caecal valve, colon.

Shingles (herpes zoster)
Shingles is a condition of the peripheral nerves caused by the herpes virus. It is the adult form of chicken pox and is extremely painful, causing inflammation of the nerve endings and blisters on the skin. It is highly contagious and should not be treated when acute.
Direct: treat the reflex of the area most affected
Associated: lymphatic system, spleen, solar plexus.

Stress, tension and insomnia
All reflexology treatments will help these problems but focus on the head, brain, solar plexus, spine and hormonal system is most important.

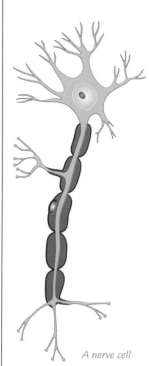
A nerve cell

THE ENDOCRINE SYSTEM

Hormonal problems affect the whole body so a general treatment will help restore balance. Particular attention should be paid to the pituitary gland which controls hormonal activity.

General treatment
Direct: the pituitary gland
Associated: thyroid, parathyroids, adrenal glands.

Thyroid problems
e.g. thyrotoxicosis (overactive thyroid) or myxoedema (underactive thyroid)
Direct: thyroid
Associated: pituitary, neck.

Goitre
(swelling of the thyroid gland)
Direct: thyroid
Associated: pituitary and adrenal glands, ovaries or testes.

Adrenal gland disorders
The adrenal glands are important for sex hormone problems, stress, imbalances of salt and water in the body, kidney conditions and blood pressure problems.
Direct: adrenal glands
Associated: pituitary, thyroid and parathyroid glands, ovaries or testes, uterus or prostate.

Reflexes of the endocrine system

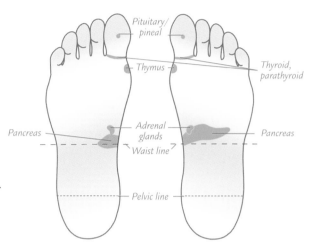

Diabetes mellitus
A condition which is caused by a problem with the pancreas. Insufficient insulin, a hormone which regulates blood sugar levels, is produced leading to hyperglycaemia (too much sugar in the blood) which can be toxic and even fatal.
Direct: pancreas
Associated: adrenal and pituitary glands, kidneys, liver, eyes.

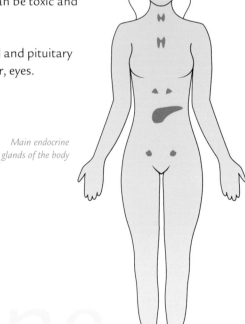

Main endocrine glands of the body

Endocrine

THE REPRODUCTIVE SYSTEM

Reflexes of the reproductive system

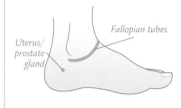

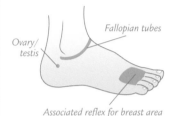

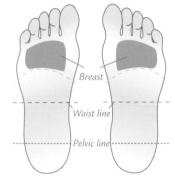

Uterus/prostate gland · Fallopian tubes · Ovary/testis · Fallopian tubes · *Associated reflex for breast area* · Breast · Waist line · Pelvic line

Breast lumps

Many breast lumps are caused by infected ducts and blocked lymph nodes.
Direct: breast
Associated: lymphatic system, pituitary, thyroid, adrenals, ovary.

Pelvic inflammatory disease

A bacterial infection of the organs of the pelvis: the ovaries, Fallopian tubes and uterus. It causes excessive vaginal discharge and pain after menstruation.
Direct: ovaries, uterus, Fallopian tubes
Associated: adrenal glands, pituitary, thyroid, lymphatic system, groin, pelvic muscles.

Female

Several conditions affect the female reproductive system, most of which are caused by hormones: premenstrual tension (irritability, depression, fluid retention, painful breasts, headaches, emotional and nervous tension); painful periods (dysmenorrhoea); heavy periods (menorrhagia); absence of menstruation (amenorrhoea); endometriosis (the lining of the womb grows outside the womb, on the ovaries, cervix and abdominal wall and disintegrates during menstruation causing pain); menopause (hot flushes, depression, headaches, dry skin, hair and vagina, insomnia).

General treatment

Direct: ovaries, Fallopian tubes
Associated: pituitary, thyroid and adrenal glands; uterus; lymphatic system.

Infertility

Infertility prevents humans from reproducing. It can affect both men and women. Reflexology may help, especially since stress can affect fertility, but as with all conditions there are no guarantees of success.
Female
Direct: ovaries, Fallopian tubes, uterus
Associated: pituitary, thyroid, adrenal glands, spinal reflexes.
Male
Direct: testes, prostate gland
Associated: pituitary, thyroid, adrenal glands.

Male reproductive system

The male reproductive system is affected by prostate problems, infertility and ureter/urinary infections.
Direct: testes, prostate gland
Associated: pituitary, thyroid, adrenals, bladder, lower spine, ureter tube, kidneys.

Reproductive

THE DIGESTIVE SYSTEM

Indigestion

Often caused by stress, or nervousness, indigestion is the failure of the digestive system to digest food. Symptoms include pain, heartburn and flatulence.
Direct: stomach
Associated: diaphragm, solar plexus, adrenal glands, liver, gall bladder, intestines.

Flatulence

Excess gas in the stomach and intestines.
Direct: small intestine, stomach, ileo-caecal valve
Associated: liver, gall bladder, pancreas.

Ulcers

A peptic ulcer is an erosion or lesion in the mucous membranes of the digestive tract. May occur in the mouth (apthous ulcer), oesophagus (oesophageal ulcer), duodenum (duodenal ulcer) or stomach (gastric ulcer).
Direct: stomach, duodenum (part of the digestive tract affected).
Associated: solar plexus, diaphragm, adrenal glands.

Reflexes of the digestive system

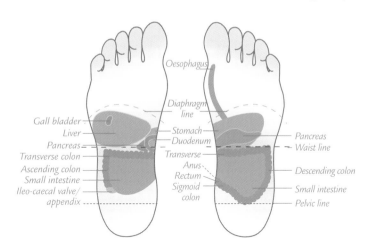

Colitis

Inflammation of the large intestine. Symptoms include abdominal pain, diarrhoea and constipation.
Direct: large intestine
Associated: solar plexus, adrenal glands, liver, gall bladder.

Diverticulitis

Inflammation of the diverticula (sacs in the intestine) especially in the colon.
Direct: all colon reflexes
Associated: diaphragm, solar plexus, liver, gall bladder, adrenal glands, lower spine.

Hernia

Rupture, in which an organ pushes through the surface of the structures which usually hold it in. Often affects the stomach.
Direct: stomach (for stomach hernia)
Associated: diaphragm, solar plexus, adrenal glands.

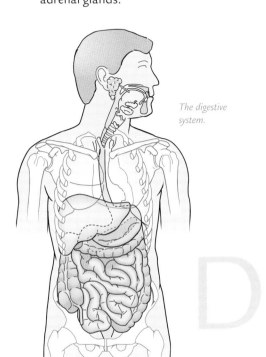

The digestive system.

Digestive

Constipation

Infrequent, difficult or painful bowel movements.

Direct: large intestine
Associated: small intestine, liver, gall bladder, solar plexus, adrenal glands, lower spine.

Diarrhoea

Frequent, liquid bowel movements.

Direct: colon reflexes
Associated: liver, adrenal glands, solar plexus.

Irritable bowel syndrome (IBS)

Abdominal pain, alternating bouts of constipation and diarrhoea; often caused by stress.

Direct: large intestine
Associated: small intestine, liver, gall bladder, pancreas, solar plexus, adrenal glands, lower spine.

Cirrhosis of the liver

Chronic damage to the liver, often caused by excessive alcohol consumption.

Direct: liver
Associated: pancreas, all glands.

Gall stones

Like kidney stones, gall stones form from deposits such as calcium and cholesterol. Whilst in the gall bladder they are usually not painful but if they move into the bile duct they can cause severe pain.

Direct: liver, gall bladder
Associated: thyroid, parathyroid, solar plexus.

Food allergies

Allergies are usually caused by the digestive tract becoming sensitised to certain substances and reacting to them. They may occur anywhere in the digestive system and can also affect the skin.

Direct: digestive tract
Associated: adrenal glands, solar plexus, spleen.

Hepatitis

Inflammation of the liver, causing jaundice and liver enlargement. Several types exist.

Direct: liver
Associated: lymphatic system, spleen, gall bladder.

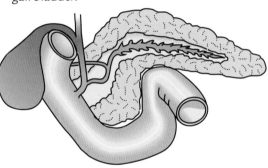

Digestive

THE RESPIRATORY SYSTEM

Colds and coughs
A general treatment is the best approach.

Sinusitis
Infection or inflammation of the sinuses which may cause headaches.
Direct: sinuses, head, face, eyes
Associated: ileo-caecal valve, adrenal glands, lymphatic system.

Hay fever
Allergic rhinitis (congested nose and sinuses) caused by allergy to certain pollens.
Direct: sinuses, head, face, eyes
Associated: ileo-caecal valve, adrenal glands, lymphatic system, lungs, spleen, solar plexus.

Bronchitis
Inflammation of the bronchial tubes. Symptoms include coughing, shortness of breath and sore chest.
Direct: lungs, bronchi
Associated: solar plexus, diaphragm, adrenal glands, ileo-caecal valve.

Asthma
A breathing condition that causes shortness of breath, wheezing and coughing. Often caused by allergies, common in children; attacks may be caused by emotional stress and nervous tension.
Direct: lungs, bronchi
Associated: solar plexus, diaphragm, adrenal glands, ileo-caecal valve, cervical and thoracic spine, pituitary, thyroid, heart.

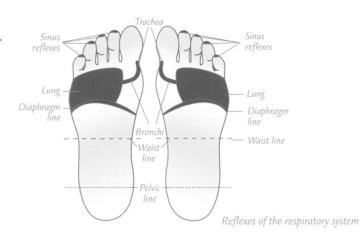

Reflexes of the respiratory system

Emphysema
The loss of elasticity in the alveoli of the lungs causes coughing, wheezing and shortness of breath. Affects the elderly.
Direct: lungs, bronchi
Associated: solar plexus, diaphragm, adrenal glands, ileo-caecal valve, lymphatic system.

Pneumonia
Inflammation of the lungs caused by infection. Symptoms include cough, chest pain, fever, fatigue.
Direct: lungs, bronchi
Associated: solar plexus, diaphragm, adrenal glands, spleen, lymphatic system.

Pleurisy
Inflammation of the pleural lining of the lungs. Causes chest pain, cough, shortness of breath.
Direct: lungs, bronchi
Associated: solar plexus, diaphragm, adrenal glands, lymphatic system.

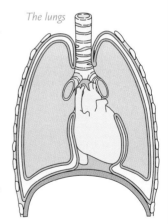

The lungs

Respiratory

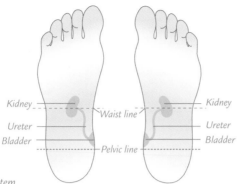

Kidney
Waist line
Ureter
Bladder
Pelvic line
Kidney
Ureter
Bladder

Reflexes of the urinary system

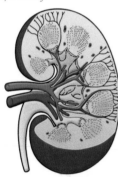

Cross-section of a kidney

Urinary infections may cause kidney damage and are therefore very dangerous. In the first instance medical advice should be sought if there is any suspicion of infection. The following conditions affect the urinary system:

Cystitis

Inflammation of the bladder.
Direct: bladder, ureter, kidneys
Associated: lymphatic system, groin, adrenal glands, solar plexus.

Urethritis

The spread of cystitis infection to the urethra.
Direct: bladder, ureter, kidneys

Associated: lymphatic system, groin, adrenal glands, solar plexus.

Nephritis or Bright's disease

Inflammation of the kidney.
Direct: bladder, ureter, kidneys
Associated: lymphatic system, groin, adrenal glands, solar plexus.

Incontinence (and bed-wetting)

The bladder muscles are weakened and cannot retain urine.
Direct: bladder, ureter, kidneys
Associated: adrenal glands (aid muscle tone), lower spine, prostate (in older men).

Kidney stones

Caused by deposits of various substances, including uric acid and calcium in the kidney. Often a result of too much calcium in the diet and lack of fluids.
Direct: bladder, ureter, kidneys
Associated: adrenal glands, diaphragm, solar plexus, parathyroids.

NB Reflexology may aid recovery but is NO substitute for medical treatment of the urinary system.

OTHER REFLEXES

Eye problems

Treating the eyes can be beneficial for infections and inflammations such as conjunctivitis, cataracts and glaucoma.
Direct: eyes
Associated: neck, cervical spine, face, kidneys, adrenal glands, lymphatic system (especially head and neck).

Ears

Reflexology can help ear infections, tinnitus (persistent ringing or buzzing in the ears) and Ménière's disease (recurrent bouts of dizziness and tinnitus).

Direct: ears
Associated: eustachian tubes, neck, cervical spine, head, sinuses, solar plexus, adrenal glands, lymphatic system.
NB Chronic, terminal and progressive illnesses such as cancers, multiple sclerosis and Parkinson's disease will often respond to reflexology treatment although medical advice should always be sought. The treatment can often make patients more comfortable, improving excretion and bowel/bladder control and reducing pain.

You now know how to treat many medical and non-medical conditions through reflexology.

7 Consultation, treatment & case studies

In Brief

A reflexology treatment consists of using the techniques described in this book to promote good health and relaxation. In order to do this a reflexologist must know how to consult with the person receiving treatment to find out as much as possible about their health and lifestyle. This chapter explains consultation techniques and required equipment, possible reactions to treatment, when not to treat and how to read the feet. It is also important that the reflexologist maintains a hygienic working environment and presents a professional image. Throughout this section the person receiving treatment will be referred to as the client.

PROFESSIONALISM

Your appearance should confirm to your clients that you are a professional and qualified therapist and should give them the confidence to enable them to relax, knowing that they are safe in your hands. Within the first fifteen seconds of meeting, your client will make a number of judgements about you and your abilities, all of which will be based on your attitude and your appearance. For example, if you look untidy and dishevelled a new client may make the assumption that the service you will provide to them is going to be slapdash and careless. If, though, you look neat and well groomed, a new client is much more likely to assume that your treatments will be careful, competent and professional.

To ensure that you look professional throughout your working day you need to pay careful attention to the following:

1. Personal hygiene

Personal hygiene is a key element of professional presentation. Use a deodorant or anti-perspirant to prevent body odour. Check that your breath is fresh on a regular basis throughout the day. Also ensure that your hair is clean and tied back off the collar and face and that your nails are short, clean and without nail polish.

2. Uniform

A clean and freshly ironed uniform is essential to presenting a professional appearance. If you are working in a clinic you will be expected to wear professional work wear. If wearing white at work you will almost certainly need at least three uniforms; one to wear, one to wash and one to keep at work as a spare just in case you have an accident.

Nothing looks more untidy or unprofessional than a white uniform that is marked with splashes or stains. It's worth noting that, for reasons of hygiene, many employers will expect you to wear tights or stockings, even during the hot summer months. If you wear tights, do make sure that they are plain and a natural colour. If you are wearing trousers you should choose full, flat shoes and socks of the same colour. It is important always to make sure that you look neat and well groomed.

3. Hair

Hair must be clean and must be tied back from your face so that it doesn't flop forward onto your face, or rest on your collar. Tied back hair will be cooler and more comfortable for you, and will also be more hygienic for the client.

4. Nails and hands

Nails and hands must be kept scrupulously clean. Nails should be neatly trimmed, as this is essential to perform the reflexology techniques such as thumb walking correctly. The client should feel the pressure of the treatment and not sharp nails pressing into their skin. Nails should also be unvarnished.

5. Perfume

Heavy perfume should be avoided as some clients may find strong odours unpleasant, or may even be allergic to certain fragrances.

6. Shoes

Shoes should be practical and, above all, comfortable as you will be wearing them throughout the working day. Your shoes should have closed toes and heels, and must be flat. As you are likely to be on your feet for long hours it's a good idea to ensure that you have a suitable pair that you can change into halfway through the day. This will help to keep your feet fresh and comfortable. It's also a good idea to have spare socks or tights to hand so that you can change those as well if you need to.

7. Jewellery

Jewellery must be kept to a plain wedding band and small stud earrings. Dangling earrings, bangles and rings must be avoided at all times as they are unhygienic and may even injure your clients. Wristwatches should be removed and left in a safe place until the end of the day, but fob watches may be worn on your uniform.

KEY POINT

Never, ever, chew gum or suck sweets whilst talking to, or working with, a client. This applies throughout the premises and, if you want to maintain the best impression with your clients, outside the premises as well

CHECKLIST

This checklist is a set of quick professional appearance checks that you can run through at the start of the day and before each client.

Before you meet your client
CHECK THAT:

- your personal hygiene is beyond question
- your uniform is spotless
- your hair is clean and neatly tied back from your face and collar
- your hands are freshly washed, and your nails are clean, neatly trimmed and filed and unvarnished
- you are not wearing heavy perfume
- your shoes are comfortable and clean, your socks are clean and your tights are not holed or laddered
- your jewellery is, at most, a plain wedding band and/or a pair of stud earrings.

A word about punctuality

Your client is entitled to expect that when they arrive for their appointment their therapist will be ready and available to begin the treatment. If you are late and keep your client waiting this sends a clear message that you do not consider them to be your number one priority. Many clients, quite rightly, will feel upset and irritated if their treatment doesn't start on time.

Also, your employer will expect you to complete a treatment within a commercially acceptable time. For example, in most clinics or spas, it is considered to be commercially acceptable to provide a reflexology treatment lasting for approximately one hour, and the price set for that treatment will be based on the cost of one hour of the reflexologist's time, plus the cost of clinic overheads such as lighting, heating, products used and so on. If, though, the reflexologist spends longer than an hour providing the treatment this will have an effect on the business – if fewer clients than expected are treated during the course of a day this means less money going into the till. This, in turn, will affect the employer's profits, and their ability to keep the business running successfully. In addition, clients often have busy schedules and plan carefully to fit a complementary therapy treatment into an hour. If the reflexologist draws out the treatment so that it takes longer than an hour, this can have a knock-on effect on the client's plans for the rest of the day, and make them late for other appointments. What should have been a soothing and relaxing experience can, if it takes too long, turn into a frustrating and irritating event, which spoils the remainder of the client's day. This is not good for the reputation of either the individual therapist, or the business. Keeping to time is an important part of professionalism. If you find that you are

Note:

- being professional is about earning and keeping the trust of your clients
- your appearance should confirm to your clients that you are a professional therapist whose personal hygiene and presentation is beyond question
- You should know the time allocated for each treatment, and stick to it
- if, for any reason, you have to keep a client waiting make sure that you apologise sincerely, and assure them that the delay was unavoidable and will not happen again
- if you find that you are running late on appointments, think about why it happens, and address the issue so that the delay is not repeated.

regularly running late with clients – which means keeping the next client waiting – you need to reflect on why this is happening, so that you can address the problem. These points also apply if you are self-employed or running your own complementary therapies center.

Some tips that can help you keep to time are to make sure that you do not:

- draw appointments out by chatting too much
- forget to keep an eye on the clock
- overestimate how much you can do in a given time.

Always remember that, after one client leaves, you will need a few minutes in which to prepare the treatment room – and yourself – for the next client.

THE PROFESSIONAL ENVIRONMENT

As well as making sure that your own appearance is immaculate, it's vital that you ensure that your treatment room, and everything in it, is spotlessly clean, neat, tidy and ready for the client's treatment. Needless to say, no client wants to find themselves in a treatment room which looks untidy or unhygienic. And, from the client's point of view, nothing appears less professional than settling down for a treatment only to find that the therapist has to leave the room to gather extra supplies such as towels or treatment products.

CHECKLIST

As one client leaves and BEFORE the next client arrives CHECK THAT:

- the treatment room is spotlessly clean, neat and tidy
- you have opened windows to allow in fresh air (if possible), or used an air freshener, if necessary
- any bins are emptied before the next treatment
- your equipment trolley is clean
- you have sufficient supplies of all the products you need for the next treatment – e.g. fresh towels, tissues, cotton wool, treatment media, etc.
- any equipment you intend to use is clean (and sterilised where necessary) and in perfect working order
- you have your client's records to

hand or, for a new client, you have a new record card and foot charts ready to be completed

- you have checked around the room to make sure that, in your professional opinion, everything is in order and ready for the next client.

The client will judge the quality of the service you provide on their complete experience with you. Even if the treatment you provide is perfectly satisfactory, if a client judges that some other aspect of the environment is unacceptable – for example, unhygienic or untidy – then they'll probably look around for another clinic that provides a cleaner, more pleasant, more comfortable setting for their next treatment. In other words, you are quite likely to lose a client to another business.

Hygiene

Providing a hygienic environment is a duty we have to our clients. It is also, for your clients, an important criteria by which they will judge your services, and whether, or not, to return or to recommend you to their friends and acquaintances. Good clinic hygiene is a continuous process that will, if carried out properly, ensure that all of the treatment areas, and all equipment used within it, are clean and free from

contamination. Preventing infection means ensuring that microorganisms (organisms that are so small they cannot be seen with the naked eye) such as bacteria, viruses and fungi do not have the opportunity to survive and multiply.

Bacteria

Bacteria are tiny, have a range of shapes – round, rod-like, or tail-like – and are only about one thousandth of a millimetre across, with millions living in a teaspoon of sour milk. While bacteria can play a beneficial role in parts of the ecosystem, may even provide antibiotics, and can help with our digestion, they are a cause of diseases ranging in severity from upset stomachs to pneumonia, tuberculosis and typhoid fever.

Viruses

Viruses are about a tenth the size of bacteria – indeed there is even one group, called bacteriophages, that feeds upon bacteria. They are responsible for some of the most devastating diseases of plants and animals. In humans, they are responsible for ailments from the common cold to herpes and HIV.

Fungi

While fungi can be seen (and enjoyed) as mushrooms, they are generally microscopic, and are another infectious organism that may affect our clients and us. They are responsible for the rising of our bread and the production of Penicillin, but they are also the causes of ringworm, thrush or candida, athletes' foot (tinea pedis) and fungal nail infections.

Parasites

Humans may play host to a number of parasites – organisms that use us for food, growth and shelter. They can live in the digestive tract as intestinal worms or on the body as lice - pediculosis capitis, corporis and pubis - which are found in the skin and hair. Another parasite, the scabies or itch mite, burrows into the skin and feeds on blood. Parasites can cause ill health through cross infection – scratching infected areas.

The client can pick up an infection from

Type of infection	Characteristics	How it spreads	Examples
Bacterial infection	Caused by bacteria, which are single-celled micro-organisms	Bacteria reproduce at the site of the infection – skin, ear, throat, vagina etc.	Skin infections such as impetigo (staphylococcus pyogens) or acne (propionibacterium acnes) Food poisoning such as salmonella
Viral infection	Caused by viruses, which are micro-organisms smaller than bacteria. Viral infections do not respond to treatment with antibiotics – penicillin etc.	Viruses reproduce inside human cells	Common cold Cold sore – herpes simplex Chicken pox – herpes zoster Wart – verrucae Hepatitis A and B HIV, which can lead to AIDS – Acquired Immune Deficiency Syndrome
Fungal infection	Caused by parasitic growth, which includes moulds, rusts, yeasts and mushrooms	Fungus is reproduced by spores	Ringworm – tinea pedis, capitis or corporus Thrush – candida albicans
Parasitic infestation	Caused by microorganisms that live on human tissue such as blood and keratin.	Spread by contact	Lice – Pediculosis capitis, corporis, pubis; Scabies (Sarcoptes scabiei)

equipment that has not been properly cleaned and sterilised, or from products that have deteriorated with age or have been contaminated by another client. To prevent the spread of bacteria, viruses, fungus or parasites within your working environment it's vital that you take the utmost care to ensure thorough sterilisation and sanitisation. This will ensure that no cross-infection occurs between one client and another. A variety of sterilisation methods and techniques are available for use in the salon. Here are some of the most suitable.

Autoclave

An autoclave is an item of electrical equipment which is used to sterilise small metal items of equipment such as, for example, scissors. When water is heated at normal atmospheric pressure, it boils at 100 degrees centigrade. The autoclave heats water under pressure, which increases the temperature at which the water boils. At a pressure of 15 pounds per square inch (psi) the boiling point of water is raised to over 120 degrees centigrade – a temperature at which good sterilisation can be achieved in 20 minutes. An autoclave, especially one with an automatic timer and a pressure

TEMPERATURE REGULATOR

gauge, is simple and effective to use and economical to run. Items to be sterilised must be capable of withstanding the heat in the autoclave, and this method is very suitable for metal instruments. It is vital that all items are washed or wiped prior to being placed in the autoclave to ensure that all surfaces are free to be cleansed.

Disinfectant liquids and solutions

We are all familiar with the use of disinfectant liquids and solutions in the home, and appropriate products have a valuable role to play in the hygiene and safety of our clinics. In clinic use, a disinfectant must be effective, economical to use and inoffensive. Typical professional products are either chemical disinfectants that may require dilution according to their instructions for use, or alcohol-based disinfectants that may be used in the form of liquids, wipes, or gel-based hand washes. Examples include products such as Barbicide, or Milton.

Before using any disinfectant product remember to:

- select an appropriate product for the use to which you are putting it
- clean small tools before disinfecting
- follow the instructions
- wear appropriate safety equipment
- allow enough time for the product to work.

After use, remember that used products will be contaminated and no longer effective, and so should be disposed of carefully. Also bear in mind that some products, such as alcohol/gel hand cleansers may be flammable.

Ultraviolet radiation (UV)

Short wave ultraviolet radiation can be used to sanitise small items. The article to be sanitised must first be cleansed and then placed in a cabinet with a source of UV radiation.

The UV radiation kills micro-organisms on the surface of the article. The UV radiation is only effective on the surface of items being sanitised (as it cannot pass through them) and, as light travels in straight lines, items must be turned during the process so that all surfaces are brought into the light and out of the shadow. The process takes roughly twenty minutes, and has the added benefit of not heating the item.

Chemical sterilisers

Liquid chemical sterilisers are plastic cabinets, usually with a perforated tray on their base. Most clinic materials can be sterilised by cleaning and drying them thoroughly and then immersing them in the liquid chemical in the steriliser. After the time indicated on the chemical manufacturer's instructions (usually between 10 and 30 minutes), the items can be removed and should be thoroughly rinsed. It is very important to choose the correct chemical for your sterilisation needs. The chemical liquid requires changing after the time specified by the manufacturer, usually about 14 to 28 days. Be very careful to avoid skin contact with the chemical liquid.

CONSULTATION, TREATMENT & CASE STUDIES

Hot bead steriliser

Hot bead sterilisers are small and easy to use. They are suitable for sterilising small objects but not for brushes, plastic, sponge or glass. Tiny glass beads are contained in a protective insulated case and heated to between 190 and 300°C (375-570°F) as indicated by the manufacturer. Sterilisation takes between 1 and 10 minutes

How infections spread

Infections are spread by touch, food and water droplets in the air, and through contact with cuts and grazes and other kinds of skin abrasions. Although it is almost impossible to create a completely sterile environment, you can reduce the risk of spreading infection by:

- not treating clients who have an obvious infection or, if the area infected is small, by avoiding it
- sterilising equipment
- disposing of waste safely
- maintaining the highest standards of hygiene

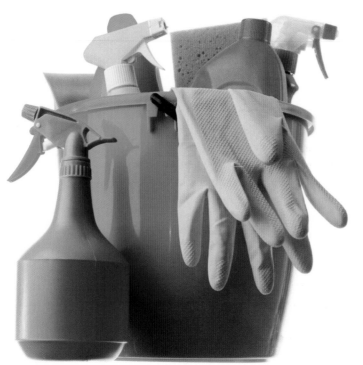

CHECKLIST

Ways to ensure a professional level of clinic hygiene

- All hard surfaces – floors, worktops, trolleys, toilets, washbasins etc – should be daily washed down with a disinfectant /sanitiser
- Clean bed linen should be used for each client, or the treatment couch or chair should be covered with clean couch roll for each new client
- Clean towels must be provided for each client, and towels should be laundered daily
- Clean towelling robes (if used) should be provided for each client
- Towels, blankets, towelling robes etc. should be laundered daily and then should be stored, clean, in a closed cupboard or laundry bin
- Waste bins should be emptied after each client and at the end of each day and disinfected
- Broken glass should be disposed of in a sharps container as the contents are collected and professionally incinerated.
- If a client has any open wounds or abrasions on their skin you should avoid touching these areas, and should make sure that the wounds are covered with a plaster before the treatment starts.
  The same applies to the therapist. Cross infection between clients can be prevented by:
- Using spatulas for treatment media removal, i.e. taking creams from pots etc
- Never using fingers to decant products
- Not scraping back into the main container any product that has been in contact with either your hands or any part of the client
- Immediately disposing of used cotton wool, tissues etc in a covered waste bin

- Washing your hands thoroughly before and after every treatment is a must.

Thorough hand washing means:

- using an antibacterial soap or bactericidal gel and warm, running water
- washing forearms, wrists, palms, backs of hands, fingers, between fingers and under fingernails
- rubbing hands together for at least 10-15 seconds
- using a clean towel, or a disposable paper towel.

CHECKLIST

Health and hygiene terms you should know

- **Antiseptic:** a chemical used to reduce the growth of bacteria
- **Asepsis:** clean and free from bacteria
- **Disinfectant:** chemical used to destroy bacteria (but not its spores)
- **Non-pathogenic Bacteria:** bacteria which is harmless or even beneficial to the human system – for example: Lactobacillus acidophilus which is found in yogurt, and Lactobacillus casei which is found in many cheeses
- **Pathogenic Bacteria:** bacteria which is harmful and which causes diseases such as, for example, cholera, typhoid and tuberculosis
- **Sanitise:** make clean
- **Sepsis:** severe illness caused by overwhelming infection of the bloodstream by toxin-producing bacteria, which can originate anywhere in the body
- **Sterilise:** make clean and completely free from bacteria and their spores

KEY POINTS

- infections caused by bacteria, viruses, fungi and parasites can easily spread from one client to another
- a client can pick up an infection from equipment that has not been properly cleaned and sterilised, or from products that have been contaminated by an infected client
- good clinic hygiene is a continuous process
- thorough hand washing is essential to good hygiene as it will prevent the spread of any infection, and keep you and your clients safe.
- Using a hand cream after washing will soothe skin and prevent dryness

PROFESSIONAL COMMUNICATION

As a reflexologist good communication skills are at the heart of your ability to relate to your clients and to deal with them professionally. By using good communication skills you will encourage your client to relax in your care.

These skills include:

- asking the right kinds of questions
- listening with attention and interest
- being comfortable with silence
- using appropriate body language.

This, in turn, will contribute to their enjoyment of the treatment and should encourage them to return.

Asking questions is one of the best ways of encouraging clients to communicate with you and give you the information you need to treat them effectively. When asking questions it's important to understand the difference between closed and open questions, so that you can ask the right kind of question at the appropriate time.

Closed questions are those to which your client will be able to give a short Yes or No answer.

Examples of closed questions include:
'Shall I open the window to let some air in?'
'Are you warm enough?'
'Would you like another blanket?'
'Have you had a facial massage before?'

Open questions can't be answered with a Yes or No. Open questions invite your client to provide information and to answer in detail.

Examples of open questions include:
'What do you hope the treatment will achieve for you?'
'Tell me about how you sleep?'
'Which parts of your back are most stiff and sore?'
'Tell me about your diet?'
'How have you been feeling since the last treatment?'

KEY POINT

Open questions are particularly useful when:

- you are meeting a client for the first time and need to take their history and complete their client record card
- you are talking to a client you have seen before and you want to find out how they responded to the last treatment you gave them and if there have been any changes, problems or improvements

Listening with attention and interest

Listening to your clients with genuine interest and attention will put your client at ease and will help to build a good professional relationship between the two of you. On the other hand, not listening to your client may persuade them that (1) you are not interested in them, (2) you don't care whether or not the treatment you provide is appropriate for their needs, and (3) you do not have a professional attitude to the work you do. Listening with attention and interest involves:

- being focused on your client throughout the time they are with you and concentrating on what they are saying
- listening without interrupting
- making eye contact with your client whilst they are speaking
- asking open questions to find out more
- remembering things your client has said to you so that at the next appointment you ask them about what they have told you – their planned holiday, family wedding, changes at work, new pet and so on

Being comfortable with silence

Some clients will enjoy talking throughout their treatment. They will regard the communication between you and them as an important part of the process, and they will happily chatter away about family and work and holidays and, probably, every other topic under the sun. Other clients, though, will regard their treatment time as a little oasis of peace and silence where they can simply relax and enjoy their therapy without having to make the effort to talk. Once you have obtained any information necessary from the client, for example: - 'How have you been?'; 'Are you warm enough?' 'Would you like more support under your knees?' - if the client lapses into silence, don't feel that you need to make small-talk conversation. This may be the only time during a busy working week when your client has the opportunity to completely relax and allow themselves to drift in peace and quiet.

However, during the reflexology treatment there will be times when you need to confirm points that you are feeling, so you may need to ask further questions if they are conscious. You will also need to note non-verbal signs of discomfort, such as facial expressions and sighs. You must be responsive to the needs of your clients.

Using appropriate body language

It is really important that you use appropriate body language with your clients, as this will put them at ease and reassure them that they are in the hands of a professional therapist.

Non-verbal communication is another phrase for body language.

The elements of good communication are being able to:

- ask the right kinds of questions
- listen with attention and interest
- be comfortable with silence
- use appropriate body language
- make yourself clearly understood.
- use open questions to gather information, whereas closed questions are used to elicit a simple 'Yes' or 'No' answer

Remember:

- listening with attention and interest will put your client at ease and make them feel valued and respected
- using positive and encouraging body language will help your client to relax and enjoy their treatment
- paying careful attention to your client's body language will help you to see when, even if they don't say anything, they are feeling uncomfortable or ill at ease with the consultation or treatment techniques i.e. pressure

CONSULTATION TECHNIQUES

Your clients have the right to expect a professional standard of care whenever they receive a treatment from you. Providing a professional standard of care involves:

- assessing the client's needs fully
- designing a treatment plan/programme to meet those needs
- recognising contraindictions
- taking account of your client's need for modesty and privacy
- not making false claims
- only providing those therapies in which you are fully trained and qualified
- not offering a diagnosis of any kind
- performing and adapting a treatment to meet the needs of the client
- documenting treatments in a confidential manner and storing records securely

Before beginning a reflexology treatment, or a series of treatments, the reflexologist will need to talk to the client in order to find out why they have come, e.g. is it for a medical condition, for a psychological problem (anxiety, depression) or simply for relaxation? In order to discuss this, it helps if the clients feel relaxed and, since relaxation is also an important part of the whole treatment, the consultation can be a useful way to help both reflexologist and client to feel comfortable with each other. It also gives the reflexologist a chance to:

- find out what the client expects
- assess client suitability for treatment
- explain the treatment and the possible effects (i.e. dispelling any unrealistic expectations)
- find out if there are any contraindications
- discuss possible contra-actions
- recommend the most suitable method of treatment, using hands or feet

- agree the treatment plan with the client
- choose and recommend suitable treatment media and methods of use.
- ask the client (or appointed advocate) to sign to consent to the treatment
- refer client to another practitioner if necessary
- fill out consultation forms.

The following topics should be covered by a consultation:

- personal details: name, address, telephone number, date of birth, GP's name and address
- medical background: medicines being taken (prescription and non-prescription medicines); medical conditions (any contraindications or problems should be referred; whatever the background a disclaimer form should be sent to a GP for confirmation that reflexology is approved); previous illnesses or hereditary diseases; operations; allergies
- diet and other factors: eating habits, fluid and alcohol consumption, smoker or non-smoker, sleep problems (like insomnia)
- stress levels: at work, home, in relationships with family and colleagues.

Reasons for treatment

- It is important to find out if the client is taking any medication (prescription or non-prescription) as the treatment may interact adversely or counteract the medication in some way, as in the case of insulin-dependent diabetics, or those clients taking drugs that thin the blood who may bruise more easily.
- discussion with the client during the consultation will enable you to determine their needs in respect of their health and well being. By ascertaining the client's expectations,

Client Consultation Form – Reflexology

College Name:
College Number:
Student Name:
Student Number:
Date:

Client Name:
Address:

Profession:
Tel. No: Day
          Eve

PERSONAL DETAILS
Age group: ❏ Under 20 ❏ 20-30 ❏ 30-40 ❏ 40-50 ❏ 50-60 ❏ 60+
Lifestyle: ❏ Active ❏ Sedentary
Last visit to the doctor:
GP Address:
No. of children (if applicable):
Date of last period (if applicable):

CONTRAINDICATIONS REQUIRING MEDICAL PERMISSION – in circumstances where medical permission cannot be obtained clients must give their informed consent in writing prior to treatment (select where/if appropriate):

❏ Pregnancy
❏ Cardiovascular conditions (thrombosis, phlebitis, hypertension, hypotension, heart conditions)
❏ Haemophilia
❏ Any condition already being treated by a GP or another complementary practitioner
❏ Medical oedema
❏ Osteoporosis
❏ Arthritis
❏ Nervous/Psychotic conditions
❏ Epilepsy
❏ Recent operations
❏ Diabetes
❏ Asthma

❏ Any dysfunction of the nervous system (e.g. Multiple sclerosis, Parkinson's disease, Motor neurone disease)
❏ Trapped/Pinched nerve (e.g. sciatica)
❏ Inflamed nerve
❏ Cancer
❏ Spastic conditions
❏ Kidney infections
❏ Whiplash
❏ Slipped disc
❏ When taking prescribed medication
❏ Acute rheumatism
❏ Undiagnosed pain

CONTRAINDICTIONS THAT RESTRICT TREATMENT (select where/if appropriate):

❏ Fever
❏ Contagious or infectious diseases
❏ Under the influence of recreational drugs or alcohol
❏ Diarrhoea and vomiting
❏ Pregnancy (first trimester)
❏ Skin diseases
❏ Localised swelling
❏ Inflammation
❏ Varicose veins
❏ Cuts
❏ Bruises

❏ Abrasions
❏ Scar tissues (2 years for major operation and 6 months for a small scar)
❏ Sunburn
❏ Hormonal implants
❏ Haematoma
❏ Recent fractures (minimum 3 months)
❏ Conditions/disorders of feet/hands
❏ Menstruation
❏ Disorders/conditions of hands/feet/nails

WRITTEN PERMISSION REQUIRED BY:
❏ GP/Specialist ❏ Informed consent
Either of which should be attached to the consultation form.

PERSONAL INFORMATION (select if/where appropriate):

Muscular/Skeletal problems: ❏ Back ❏ Aches/Pain ❏ Stiff joints ❏ Headaches
Digestive problems: ❏ Constipation ❏ Bloating ❏ Liver/Gall bladder ❏ Stomach
Circulation: ❏ Heart ❏ Blood pressure ❏ Fluid retention ❏ Tired legs ❏ Varicose veins ❏ Cellulite ❏ Kidney problems ❏ Cold hands and feet
Gynaecological: ❏ Irregular periods ❏ P.M.T ❏ Menopause ❏ H.R.T ❏ Pill ❏ Coil
Other:
Nervous system: ❏ Migraine ❏ Tension ❏ Stress ❏ Depression

Immune system: ❏ Prone to infections ❏ Sore throats ❏ Colds ❏ Chest ❏ Sinuses

Regular antibiotic/medication taken? ❏ Yes ❏ No
If yes, which ones:
Herbal remedies taken? ❏ Yes ❏ No
If yes, which ones:
Ability to relax: ❏ Good ❏ Moderate ❏ Poor
Sleep patterns: ❏ Good ❏ Poor ❏ Average No. of hours
Do you see natural daylight in your workplace? ❏ Yes ❏ No
Do you work at a computer? ❏ Yes ❏ No If yes how many hours
Do you eat regular meals? ❏ Yes ❏ No
Do you eat in a hurry? ❏ Yes ❏ No
Do you take any food/vitamin supplements? ❏ Yes ❏ No
If yes, which ones:
How many portions of each of these items does your diet contain per day?
Fresh fruit: Fresh vegetables: Protein: source?
Dairy produce: Sweet things: Added salt: Added sugar:
How many units of these drinks do you consume per day?
Tea: Coffee: Fruit juice: Water: Soft drinks: Others:
Do you suffer from food allergies? ❏ Yes ❏ No
Do you suffer from eating disorders? Bingeing? ❏ Yes ❏ No Overeating? ❏ Yes ❏ No
Under eating? ❏ Yes ❏ No
Do you smoke? ❏ No ❏ Yes How many per day?
Do you drink alcohol? ❏ No ❏ Yes How many units per day?
Do you exercise? ❏ None ❏ Occasional ❏ Irregular ❏ Regular Types:
What is your skin type? ❏ Dry ❏ Oily ❏ Combination ❏ Mature ❏ Young
Do you suffer/have you suffered from: ❏ Dermatitis ❏ Acne ❏ Eczema ❏ Psoriasis

❏ Allergies ❏ Hay Fever ❏ Asthma ❏ Skin cancer
Stress level: 1–10 (10 being the highest)
At work   At home

Reason for treatment:

REFLEXOLOGY FOOT CHART
Client's name: Date:

REFLEXOLOGY FOOT CHART
Client's name: Date:

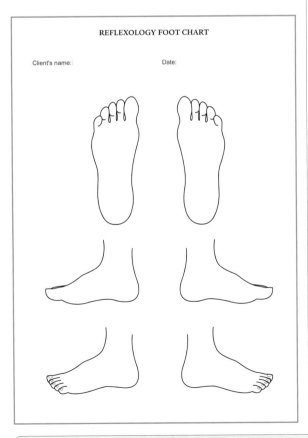

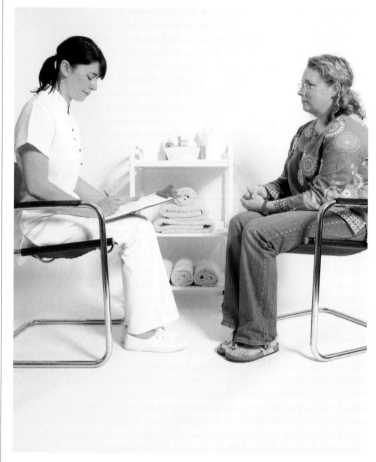

Personal details, medical background, dietary factors and lifestyle and environment information as discussed above can thus be recorded easily and clearly. All information should remain confidential and be stored in line with current data protection legislation.

Not making false claims

As a professional you are required to work within the law. The Trades Description Act 1968 relates to the false description of goods and making misleading statements to members of the public. What this means for you, as a reflexologist, is that:

- if a manufacturer makes a misleading statement with regard to their product – for example, 'Will burn away all unsightly fat overnight' – and you repeat the misleading statement to a client, you will be liable to prosecution
- if you make false claims about pricing – for example, 'This product is a great deal because we're offering it at £10 (half price) this week' when it actually cost £15 last week you will be liable to prosecution.

Imagine, for example, a client asks for a reflexology treatment and says 'I've heard this is really good and helps you lose weight and look years younger.' If this is not true you will only remain within the law if you, for example,
(1) agree that it is a popular treatment (providing that statement is true), or (2) agree that you've heard some clients have had good results (providing that statement is true and that the client could certainly try it for him/herself and see what they think of the results. It is fine to say what you are aiming to achieve with your treatment or therapy, and what you hope might happen as a result. But it is really important not to make promises about the outcome the client should expect.

you will be able to plan a suitable treatment programme incorporating the most beneficial techniques, possible treatment/problem areas, and treatment media.

- after carefully discussing and recommending a treatment plan or program, ask the client to sign the consultation form to consent before beginning the treatment. In circumstances, such as in a care environment, where the clients are unable to sign themselves, a legally appointed companion or advocate should sign to consent to the treatment on their behalf.

Consultation forms

In order to keep clear records of all treatment cases, a standard consultation form should be used, examples of which are shown on the previous page.

If you make unrealistic or untrue claims you are breaking the law and, almost certainly, your client will be disappointed and unhappy when your false promises fail to materialise.

To stay within the law you must:

- **NOT** supply information that is in any way untrue or misleading
- **NOT** falsely describe or make false statements about either products or services
- **NOT** make false contrasts between previous prices and current prices
- **NOT** claim that a product or service is being sold at 'half price' unless the product or service has been offered at full price for at least 28 days prior to the 'half price' sale.

Only providing those therapies in which you are fully trained and qualified working within your own scope of practice

As a professional it is vital that you recognise your role and its limits. From time to time a client may ask – or you may feel tempted to offer – advice or treatment in an area in which you are not trained or qualified.

Don't go beyond your own limits. Always stick to what you know, and remember that you are in a relationship of trust with your client. If you go beyond the limits of what you can or should do, you are breaking that trust and may also be risking harm to your client. Always remember that if a client in your care is harmed then your own career and reputation may be damaged, possibly beyond repair.

In a situation where a client asks you for a treatment which you are not able to provide don't hesitate to refer them on to a more experienced therapist. In these circumstances, always make sure that you have the client's permission before passing on any details of the client's treatment and health.

Not offering a diagnosis of any kind

In your career as a reflexologist there are almost certainly bound to be times when a client will ask 'Will you have a look at this ... what do you think it is?' The client might be asking about a lump or a mole, a lesion, a patch of dry skin, a rash .... there are any number of different possibilities.

No matter what you think or what you suspect, it's vital to remember that you are not trained or qualified to diagnose. Regardless of the circumstances do not offer your opinion but do suggest that the client consults their own doctor. You can do this without alarming the client by saying something like 'To be honest, I really don't know what it is. If I were you I'd make an appointment to see your doctor or your practice nurse ... they'll be able to have a look and tell you what it is.'.

Referral procedures

There will be occasions when you are unsure whether to proceed with a treatment. These instances include the listed contraindications and also any other medical conditions, skin problems or contraindications to medication about which you are uncertain. The best way to approach this is to refer the client to their GP so that they can check whether reflexology is advisable. It is not the job of the reflexologist to diagnose medical problems or decide if a condition is treatable — in fact the code of conduct of many relevant associations such as the CThA (Complementary Therapists Association) states that diagnosis is not allowed. If in doubt, refer the client to a qualified medical practitioner. If the reflexologist feels unable or unqualified to help the client, they may need to refer them to another complementary therapist such as an osteopath or acupuncturist. If the client has requirements outside of the scope of a complementary therapy practice, they may need referring to counselling services, or other voluntary or statutory services such as Social Services or voluntary advice centres.

How to carry out a consultation

The client must feel relaxed enough to explain the problem or reason that has made them come for a reflexology treatment. The reflexologist needs to use their professional communication skills to gain as much useful information from the client as they can before the treatment, in order to assess and design a suitable treatment programme.

First, you need a space to consult in. A private, comfortable area, where there will be no interruptions would be suitable. Try to arrange the room/space in an open, inviting way and ensure that your own body language is positive and open, e.g. sit facing the client, at the same height, not behind a table or desk.

How to find out what you need to know

Many clients consulting with a reflexologist for the first time may be nervous and unwilling to reveal much information about why they have come, either through embarrassment, anxiety or shyness. An open and relaxed person will usually volunteer the required information but with more reticent clients the reflexologist needs to know how to ask a question as well as how to listen to the answers.

- Start with general questions or, if you want a prompt or sense a particularly reticent client, use the form/record card as a starting point. Once the easy questions (name, address, date of birth etc) have been tackled, the more difficult ones about treatment and contraindications won't seem so daunting — the client will be in the rhythm of responding to your questions and will know what to expect.

- Ask open, not closed questions: no one likes to examine their own habits so it is best to address the questions in as unthreatening a manner as possible.

It is also important to explain why a therapist needs such information (e.g. to prevent contraindications or exacerbating existing conditions).

- In order to instil trust, use your own body language to encourage and aid responses: nodding, smiling and leaning forward all communicate interest as does keeping eye contact. Looking away frequently, fidgeting or staring blankly will communicate nervousness and/or lack of interest which will not help the client to feel confident in your abilities or your interest in them. Remember that, as a reflexologist, you are there to help the client: if you are unfriendly, anxious or uncommunicative the client is likely to pick up on this and react in a similar way.

- Be confident, enthusiastic and professional.

- Communicate your own belief and trust in the treatment: this will help the client to believe in it and will improve the psychological and physiological effects of the treatment.

- Reassure the client that everything discussed will remain completely confidential and make sure that you never break this confidence.

- Treat everyone equally: if you cannot avoid bringing racist or sexist prejudices to the consultation room reflexology is not the profession for you.

You now know how to find out necessary information from the client. The next section explains when treatment is not advised.

CONTRAINDICATIONS

When not to treat

There are many reflexologists who would argue that the treatment is completely safe and without contraindication. However, others advise caution especially for those new to the therapy. The following is a list of possible contraindications. However, it should be stressed that if, after an initial consultation, there is any doubt about the client's suitability for treatment, the treatment should not be continued until approval has been received from the client's GP or the client has signed an informed consent form.

In circumstances where written medical permission cannot be obtained, clients must sign an informed consent form stating that the treatment has been fully explained to them and confirm that they are willing to proceed without permission from their GP

- Pregnancy
- Cardio vascular conditions (thrombosis, phlebitis, hypertension, hypotension, heart conditions). Reflexology stimulates the circulation which may cause complications
- Haemophilia
- Any condition already being treated by a GP or another complementary practitioner
- Medical oedema
- Osteoporosis
- Arthritis
- Nervous/Psychotic conditions: reflexology may trigger emotional instability
- Epilepsy: treatment may stimulate an attack
- Recent operations
- Diabetes: reflexology can affect insulin levels
- Asthma
- Any dysfunction of the nervous system (e.g. Multiple sclerosis, Parkinson's disease, Motor neurone disease)
- Bell's palsy
- Trapped/Pinched nerve (e.g. sciatica)
- Inflamed nerve
- Cancer
- Spastic conditions
- Kidney infections
- Whiplash
- Slipped disc
- When taking prescribed medication
- Acute rheumatism
- Undiagnosed pain

Contraindications that restrict treatment

- Fever
- Contagious or infectious diseases
- Under the influence of recreational drugs or alcohol
- Diarrhoea and vomiting
- Pregnancy (first trimester)
- Skin diseases
- Localised swelling
- Inflammation
- Varicose veins
- Cuts
- Bruises
- Abrasions
- Scar tissues (2 years for major operation and 6 months for a small scar)
- Sunburn
- Haematoma
- Recent fractures (minimum 3 months)
- Menstruation
- Hormonal implants
- Diseases/disorders of feet/hands
- Diseases/disorders of nails

In addition reflexology should be used with extreme care on the neonate, infants, children, the elderly, or infirm. Adaptations to treatments will be required for these client groups as well as for pregnant clients, those clients with disabilities and when working in a palliative care setting.

You now know how to find out as much as possible about your client's health and how to determine if a client is suitable for reflexology. Before starting there is one last fact-finding process, known as 'reading the feet'.

READING THE FEET

The final stage of the consultation process happens on the couch, once the client is settled and barefoot. It is known as reading the feet. The consultation gives the reflexologist the opportunity to assess the client through their vocal tone, demeanour, posture, body language, and body odour in addition to the disclosure of their health and medical details. The feet provide many extra clues to the state of a person's health and lifestyle and before treatment begins the reflexologist needs to 'read' these clues and make a note of them on the consultation card or on a special foot chart. It is advisable to create an individual foot chart for each client at the beginning of treatment using a standard format as shown previously. Additional foot charts can be used at the end of each treatment to record areas treated and any other observations so that over the course of treatment the reflexologist can be aware of changes and progress and treat the client accordingly. The following should be checked and noted on the consultation form prior to beginning any reflexology treatment:

- **Local contraindications:** are there any local contraindications present such as undiagnosed pain or swelling? Restrictions to treatment may be present on the feet such as onychocryptosis, tinea pedis or unguium, which may mean that the treatment has to be performed on the hands instead;
- **Skin texture:** is the skin rough or smooth? Is the client young, with a smooth healthy skin or elderly with thin, fragile skin? What is their general skin condition – normal, dry, oily, sensitive, dehydrated? Skin type can often be an indicator of other

health issues, such as poor diet or stress. The texture of the skin may also require a particular treatment media; rather than no medium it may be easier to work on very dry, dehydrated feet with a cream specifically created for reflexology treatment;

- **hard skin**: look for patches of rough, hard or calloused skin. These may indicate postural problems if very hard and thickened in specific areas or be a sign of neglect.
- **colour**: what colour are they? Pinkish skin colour indicates good circulation whereas pale or bluish skin indicates poor circulation; very red or shiny skin indicates soreness and/or a pressure point;
- **flexibility**: are the feet easy to manoeuvre or rigid? If the feet are very stiff, this may indicate arthritis or a rigid personality;
- **muscle tone**: are the feet flabby or firm/tight? The muscle tone of the feet indicates the general muscle tone of the body;
- **temperature**: do the feet feel hot or cold? Like skin colour, temperature will indicate circulatory problems: the warmer the feet the better the circulation;
- **swelling/puffiness**: is there any swelling around the ankle, toes or joints? This indicates insufficient lymph drainage, circulation problems and/or kidney problems.
- **odour**: do the feet have a particular or unpleasant smell? Smelly feet may suggest kidney problems or could indicate skin or nail infections;
- **dampness**: are the feet dry or damp? Damp, sweaty feet may indicate a hormonal imbalance or a particularly nervous person; dry skin may be a skin condition or a sign of neglect;

damp flaky patches between the toes may be athlete's foot;

- **alignment of the feet:** How are the client's feet positioned on the couch or chair? How do the feet fall naturally when the client is relaxed? Do they roll inwards or fall outwards, or are they completely straight? May indicate postural problems or give non-verbal signs of the client's personality – i.e. rigid, relaxed.
- **shape of feet and toes:** it is worth noting the particular shape of the feet and toes. This helps to monitor diseases and disorders affecting the structure of the feet such as arthritis or improvements with corns. It is also thought by some to reflect the client's body type so long and lean clients normally have long, thin feet!
- **condition and type of nails:** are the nails dry, normal, smooth or ridged? Are they a normal pink colour, or white and flaky or yellow and thickened? Changes in nail texture may indicate systemic diseases or fungal disorders. They may require referral (in the case of severe fungal disorders) or restrict the treatment.
- **skeletal deformities:** are there any bone spurs present or problems with footwear arising from the shape of the feet?

- **arches of the feet:** does the client have high, normal or low arches? Abnormalities may indicate postural or muscular problems.

The feet should be read before beginning any treatment and changes should be noted during any ongoing treatment programme. When working on the hands, they should also be 'read' prior to a treatment, with details of the general points such as skin texture, hard skin, temperature, colour, condition and type of nails noted.

Although it is a chiropodist's job to treat the feet, the reflexologist can advise on how to improve the condition of the feet:

- **nails**: toenails should be regularly trimmed and cut straight to avoid ingrowing toenails;
- **shoes**: proper, well-fitting shoes should be worn and at home, wherever possible, the feet should be left bare without the restrictions of shoes and socks;
- **washing**: after washing the feet should be properly dried. Regular application of moisturiser can prevent hard skin developing.

For further information on conditions affecting the feet see Chapter 3.

You now know how to find out the necessary information required to give an effective and safe treatment. The next section explains the equipment that is needed and other practical considerations.

CARRYING OUT A TREATMENT

How long is a treatment?
Most treatments take around 45 minutes with 15 minutes for consultation and settling the client. A programme of between four and six weekly sessions is usual though some clients may want just one treatment and others may continue with reflexology on a regular basis.

Where should a treatment be carried out?
A treatment room which is private without risk of interruption. Fear of interruption will usually counteract the positive, relaxing benefits of the treatment. Make sure that there is a suitable ambient temperature.

Taking account of your client's need for modesty and privacy

It is fairly safe to say that, with one or two exceptions, most people (both men and women) have issues about one or more parts of their body.

For example, many women would like to have larger or smaller breasts, smaller waists, flatter tummies, thicker hair, smoother skin or daintier feet. In the same way, many men would like to be taller, or more muscular or be slimmer around the waist. The key point here is that, for some clients, the notion of removing any part of their clothes and allowing a stranger to work on unclothed areas of their body may be quite daunting. It is therefore extremely important that you take account of your client's feelings throughout any complementary therapy treatment, and in particular ensure that your client's modesty is preserved at all times.

CHECKLIST
To ensure that your client's modesty is protected at all times CHECK THAT:

- Before the treatment starts you explain to a new client **(1)** which areas of the body you will be working on and **(2)** the garments they will need to remove. Also reassure your client that they will be completely covered throughout the treatment apart from the small, specific area of the body that you will be working on at any one time.

- Allow your client to prepare alone and in complete privacy, and make sure they have a clean, unworn robe to wear as they walk to the treatment couch. If receiving a reflexology treatment as part of a spa visit for instance, they may prefer to wear swimwear and a robe whilst relaxing for the day, rather than remaining fully clothed.

- Once the client is settled on the treatment couch wrap him/her in a blanket and towels. This will preserve their modesty, keep them warm and also provide a feeling of being cosy, safe and completely covered up.

- Ensure that the client's privacy is protected at all times by making sure that no-one else can see into the treatment room. If, for some reason, another therapist enters the room during the treatment ensure that your client is fully covered so that their modesty is preserved whilst the other person is in the room. (Remember, even if the visitor is another therapist they are not your client's therapist… you are… and the client may feel embarrassed or uneasy.)

- Make sure that your client has the time and privacy to get dressed if they have been wearing a robe, or put their footwear back on before your next client arrives.

Remember, your client is entitled to be treated with the utmost respect at all times… before, during and after their treatment.

What equipment is needed?
- **a height-adjustable couch**

In order to comfortably and effectively perform a reflexology treatment a proper height-adjustable couch is recommended covered with a blanket or towel, with a pillow for the head and sometimes a rolled towel to

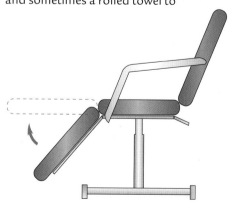

Reclining/hydraulic chair.

support the small of the back. Reclining or hydraulic chairs are also becoming popular for use during treatments. The reflexologist should sit in a height-adjustable chair, with plenty of back support, which can easily and comfortably be positioned at the end of the couch. Height adjustments will be necessary in order for the reflexologist to sit in the correct position without straining the back, shoulders, neck or arms.

- **pillows and towels for support and protection**

A pillow under the client's head will make him/her more comfortable. Rolled towels can be used under the ankles and additional support may also be required under the knees. A towel can be used to cover the foot that is not being treated in order to keep it warm.

- **treatment supplies and documentation**

It is essential to have plentiful supplies of treatment media such as cotton wool, tissues, sanitiser, powder, cornstarch or creams to finish the treatment readily available. These should be positioned to allow for safe and hygienic usage. These items must be securely stored when not in use, to prevent inappropriate access, spillages or degradation of the products. Treatment documentation such as consultation forms and foot charts should also be available, and these should be on a clipboard for ease of use during the treatment. Pens or pencils to mark the charts as the treatment progresses should also be available on the trolley. Check that pens are working before you begin a treatment!

- **bathroom**

It is helpful if both reflexologist and client go to the toilet before the treatment begins to prevent interruption. The reflexologist should cleanse the client's feet prior to starting the treatment either by bathing them in a bowl or sanitising them with a suitable sanitiser such as surgical spirit.

How do I relax the client?

In order for the client to feel relaxed, certain aspects need to be considered. As discussed above the room should be a comfortable temperature, the client's privacy should never be compromised and the reflexologist should be dressed professionally and tidily. Lighting should be bright enough for the treatment to be carried out but not harsh: fluorescent and neon lights can often be over-bright. When settling the client on the couch, ensure that they are comfortable. Some clients may wish to listen to music or talk, some may prefer silence. Remember that this is their time and you should respect their wishes — they are not paying to hear your views or personal preferences.

Are there any reactions to treatment?

Though a very gentle therapy, reflexology can have powerful emotional and physical effects. Potential reactions and contra-actions to the treatment should be discussed during the consultation in a manner that will not alarm the client. Advise them that they may suffer an increase in symptoms currently experienced, for example fatigue or muscular aches. An increase in headaches, bowel movements or in the frequency of micturition may also be experienced during the treatment programme. It is important to explain that these reactions are normal and will quickly pass, usually within 24-48 hours. Another term commonly used to describe these symptoms is healing crisis. It is useful to balance discussion of

> **Did you know?**
>
> A client's symptoms may get worse immediately after the first reflexology treatment. This is known as a healing crisis. The treatment has started to have an effect, rebalancing and resolving the problem and condition, and often the main symptoms recur before health improves and/or symptoms stop altogether. This is perfectly normal and a reflexologist should reassure their client not to be alarmed by the process.

CONSULTATION, TREATMENT & CASE STUDIES

contra-actions or a potential healing crisis with details on the benefits of the treatment; after all, you want to encourage the client to have reflexology, not put them off completely!

Common reactions to treatment include:

- a desire to urinate and/or change in colour/odour of urine
- a desire to defecate and/or change in colour/odour of faeces
- headaches
- diarrhoea
- tiredness
- nausea (especially in cases of digestive problems)
- runny nose or cough (especially if sinuses/nose/chest congestion is a problem)
- change in sleep patterns
- heightened emotional reactions
- sometimes an increase in a pain felt before treatment.

These are all normal responses to the treatment which disappear very quickly. The treatment encourages the body to cleanse itself of toxins and residues, thus helping it to heal. It is sensible to advise clients to expect such reactions and to reassure them that they are normal and there is nothing to worry about. Over a course of 4–6 treatments these responses usually settle down.

GOOD PROFESSIONAL PRACTICE

Good professional practice

It is extremely important for any reflexologist to take the following information into consideration when carrying out treatments.

- **emotions and sex**

A professional reflexologist will not allow any emotional or sexual involvement with a client to compromise the client's position. Similarly, if you feel that the client is behaving inappropriately towards you, you would be perfectly within your rights to discontinue the treatment.

- **psychology**

It is important not to become the client's counsellor. Obviously if a client feels relaxed and comfortable with the reflexologist, s/he may talk of their problems or thoughts but the reflexologist must resist the temptation to get personally involved, or offer judgements or advice. It is wise to avoid topics of conversation that may cause offence or strong feelings such as money, marriage, religion or politics (especially controversial issues like abortion, capital punishment, immigration).

You now know the practical and professional aspects of giving a reflexology treatment.

NOTE

When a client responds unfavourably to a particular treatment or product, this is called a contra-action. Examples of contra-actions to reflexology include nausea, flatulence, heavier menstrual flow or headaches.

- a contraindication is a sign, signal or symptom that tells you it would be unsafe to provide a particular kind or part of a treatment to a client.
- a contra-action is a sign or symptom that a client has responded unfavourably to a treatment or a product.
- when necessary, you should not hesitate to refer clients on to their GP, practice nurse or another professional if you suspect the client has a medical condition that needs attention.
- you should never offer a client a diagnosis, even if they ask. You are not trained or qualified to do this.
- you must always recommend only those treatments that are relevant and appropriate for the client.
- you must never offer treatments or advice outside the areas in which you are trained and qualified (scope of practice).
- you must never make false claims for the treatments you provide, or the products you use.
- you must avoid making disrespectful or damaging comments about other therapies, other therapists and other complementary therapy practices.

8 Case studies

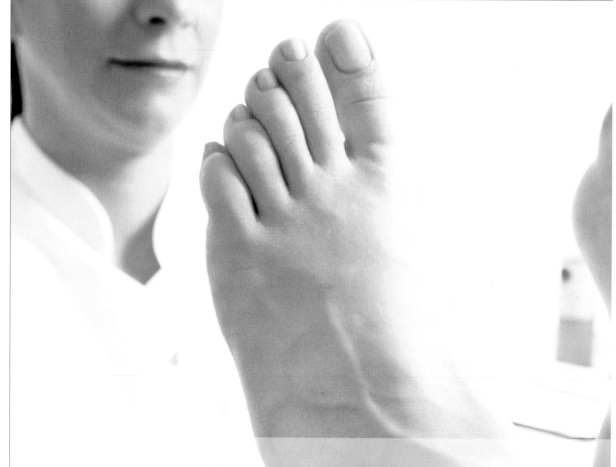

Learning objectives

The target knowledge of this chapter is:
● An example of a professional reflexology case study, including reflective practice and overall conclusion.

In Brief

Record keeping is an important part of the reflexology treatment. Maintaining confidential case studies on each client helps the therapist monitor progress and adjust the treatment programme when necessary, with each treatment providing an ever changing picture of the client's health. Therapists can also evaluate their own professional progress through the use of reflective practice. This chapter gives examples of the information recorded in a case study.

CLIENT PROFILE

Mrs GH is 52 years old. She is married and has two grown up children. She works full time as a care assistant in a nursing and residential home, where she has worked for a number of years.

She enjoys her job but finds it tiring both mentally and physically. She works on average at least 36 hours each week. She has, over the years, become quite attached to some of the residents and finds the new Matron of the home difficult to work with. This is a cause of some stress, and she feels that the levels of stress in her job have risen due to changes in management and working practices. Her diet is not particularly good and she eats some ready meals. She also smokes and drinks little or no water but quite a few cups of tea and coffee in a day.

She suffers a few health problems and thinks that some may be stress related. She has suffered psoriasis for a long time but it is getting increasingly worse, and now she has large patches on her whole body, with the exception of her face, although she has small patches in her ears. She suspects she may have a wheat allergy but has not had this diagnosed properly. She has borderline low blood pressure and a varicose vein on her lower left leg from an injury experienced 15 years ago. She had pneumonia at birth but has suffered no long term respiratory problems. She did suffer from depression after the death of her mother and subsequently took the drug valium, but has not taken it for six years. Her job involves lots of lifting and moving residents and patients. She suffers aches and pains in her back and hip region which is made worse by sitting for long periods.

Although she is friendly, she is quite shy and introverted. She watches very little television, preferring instead to read romance novels and help out with her grandchildren. She finds it hard to get to sleep at night, finding it difficult to switch off. She usually gets 6-7 hours per night, but this is often broken sleep. She does not express her stresses to her husband and bottles up problems. She sometimes gets depressed, depending on the circumstances, and finds a good cry releases some of her tension/ worries.

She also experiences regular sinus congestion and headaches, and thinks this may be linked to a wheat allergy. Her GP is recommending a course of treatment for her psoriasis to start in one month's time. This may cause liver damage, which she is worried about. She would like to try reflexology to see if it will help with the sinus congestion, help her relax and ease the psoriasis. Her family medical history seems to suggest that she is suffering from inherited problems. Her mother had circulatory problems which resulted in her death. Both her father and sister suffer from psoriasis and her brother has heart problems. Mrs GH also suffers tingling in her fingers and there is evidence of Raynaud's syndrome in her family, which she now worries that she might have. She has discussed the treatment in full with her therapist and has signed an informed consent form. The treatment and effects have been fully explained and Mrs GH is happy to proceed.

Client Consultation Form – Reflexology

ITEC

College Name:
College Number:
Student Name:
Student Number:
Date: Feb

Client Name: Mrs Gltt
Address: Dorset

Profession: Care Assistant
Tel. No: Day
                      Eve

PERSONAL DETAILS

Age group: ❏ Under 20   ❏ 20–30   ❏ 30–40   ❏ 40–50   ☑ 50–60   ❏ 60+
Lifestyle: ☑ Active   ❏ Sedentary
Last visit to the doctor: ❏ Jan
GP Address: Dorset
No. of children (if applicable): 2
Date of last period (if applicable):

CONTRAINDICATIONS REQUIRING MEDICAL PERMISSION – **in circumstances where medical permission cannot be obtained clients must give their informed consent in writing prior to treatment (select where/if appropriate):**

❏ Pregnancy
❏ Cardiovascular conditions (thrombosis, phlebitis, hypertension, hypotension, heart conditions)
❏ Haemophilia
☑ Any condition already being treated by a GP or another complementary practitioner
❏ Medical oedema
❏ Osteoporosis
❏ Arthritis
❏ Nervous/Psychotic conditions
❏ Epilepsy
❏ Recent operations
❏ Diabetes
❏ Asthma

❏ Any dysfunction of the nervous system (e.g. Multiple sclerosis, Parkinson's disease, Motor neurone disease)
❏ Trapped/Pinched nerve (e.g. sciatica)
❏ Inflamed nerve
❏ Cancer
❏ Spastic conditions
❏ Kidney infections
❏ Whiplash
❏ Slipped disc
❏ When taking prescribed medication
❏ Acute rheumatism
❏ Undiagnosed pain

CONTRAINDICTIONS THAT RESTRICT TREATMENT
(select where/if appropriate):

❏ Fever
❏ Contagious or infectious diseases
❏ Under the influence of recreational drugs or alcohol
❏ Diarrhoea and vomiting
❏ Pregnancy (first trimester)
❏ Skin diseases
❏ Localised swelling
☑ Inflammation
❏ Varicose veins
❏ Cuts
❏ Bruises

❏ Abrasions
❏ Scar tissues (2 years for major operation and 6 months for a small scar)
❏ Sunburn
❏ Hormonal implants
❏ Haematoma
❏ Recent fractures (minimum 3 months)
❏ Conditions/disorders of feet/hands
❏ Menstruation
❏ Disorders/conditions of hands/feet/nails

WRITTEN PERMISSION REQUIRED BY:

❏ GP/Specialist   ☑ Informed consent
Either of which should be attached to the consultation form.

PERSONAL INFORMATION (select if/where appropriate):

Muscular/Skeletal problems: ☑ Back ☑ Aches/Pain ☐ Stiff joints ☐ Headaches

Digestive problems: ☐ Constipation ☐ Bloating ☐ Liver/Gall bladder ☐ Stomach

Circulation: ☐ Heart ☑ Blood pressure ☐ Fluid retention ☑ Tired legs ☑ Varicose veins
☐ Cellulite ☐ Kidney problems ☐ Cold hands and feet

Gynaecological: ☐ Irregular periods ☐ P.M.T ☐ Menopause ☐ H.R.T ☐ Pill ☐ Coil
Other: *Has hormone implant regularly*

Nervous system: ☐ Migraine ☐ Tension ☑ Stress ☑ Depression
Mild depression and took valium 6 years ago after the death of her mother.

Immune system: ☐ Prone to infections ☐ Sore throats ☐ Colds ☐ Chest ☑ Sinuses
Constant congestion in the sinuses which may be due to unknown allergen

Regular antibiotic/medication taken? ☐ Yes ☑ No
If yes, which ones:

Herbal remedies taken? ☐ Yes ☑ No
If yes, which ones:

Ability to relax: ☐ Good ☑ Moderate ☐ Poor

Sleep patterns: ☐ Good ☑ Poor ☐ Average No. of hours *6*

Do you see natural daylight in your workplace? ☐ Yes ☑ No

Do you work at a computer? ☐ Yes ☑ No If yes how many hours *1*

Do you eat regular meals? ☑ Yes ☐ No

Do you eat in a hurry? ☑ Yes ☐ No

Do you take any food/vitamin supplements? ☐ Yes ☑ No
If yes, which ones:

How many portions of each of these items does your diet contain per day?
Fresh fruit: *1* Fresh vegetables: *3* Protein: *2* source? *Meat, fish, eggs*
Dairy produce: *2* Sweet things: *1* Added salt: *1* Added sugar: *0*

How many units of these drinks do you consume per day?
Tea: *2* Coffee: *5* Fruit juice: *1* Water: *0* Soft drinks: *0* Others: *0*

Do you suffer from food allergies? ☐ Yes ☑ No

Do you suffer from eating disorders? Bingeing? ☐ Yes ☑ No Overeating? ☐ Yes ☑ No
Under eating? ☐ Yes ☐ No *Mrs Gilt is unsure is sinus problems are due to food or other allergy*

Do you smoke? ☐ No ☑ Yes How many per day? *10–15*

Do you drink alcohol? ☐ No ☑ Yes How many units per day? *1*

Do you exercise? ☑ None ☐ Occasional ☐ Irregular ☐ Regular Types:

What is your skin type? ☑ Dry ☐ Oily ☐ Combination ☐ Mature ☐ Young

Do you suffer/have you suffered from: ☐ Dermatitis ☐ Acne ☐ Eczema ☑ Psoriasis
For a number of years, now getting much worse.
☑ Allergies ☐ Hay Fever ☐ Asthma ☐ Skin cancer

Stress level: 1–10 (10 being the highest)
At work *7* At home *6*

Reason for treatment: *Psoriasis, sinus congestions, headaches, stress. Mrs Gilt feels that reflexology might help with all of these conditions.*

REFLEXOLOGY FOOT CHART

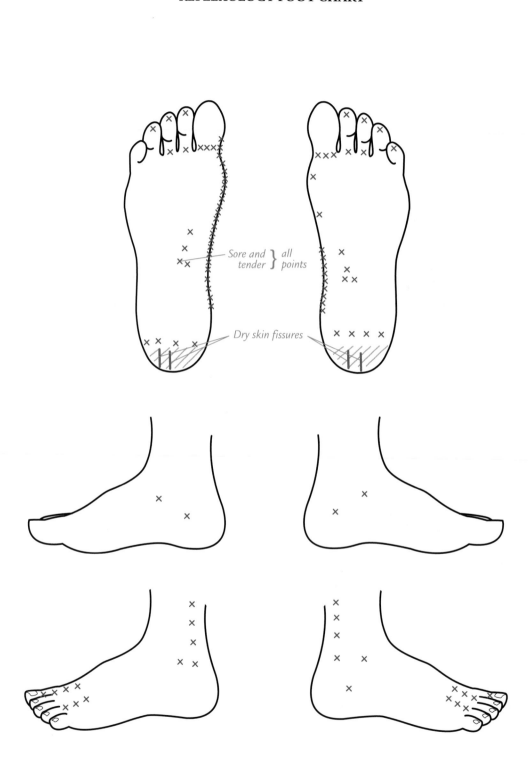

Sore and } all
tender } points

Dry skin fissures

TREATMENT 1

READING OF THE FEET

Local contraindications: none

Skin texture/areas of hard skin:
Dry, particularly the heels, which have
fissures in them

Colour: Pink on soles, normal on top

Flexibility: Good

Temperature: Cool to touch

Swelling/puffiness: None

Odour: No detectable odour

Foot position: Normal

Nail condition: Good but some slight
thickening in little toenails

Skeletal structure/arches of the feet:
Normal

Details of how the therapist conducted the treatment plan

I talked Mrs GH through the whole
treatment before getting her onto the
couch. I cleansed her feet and performed
a full foot reading. I then worked through
a whole reflexology routine to find out if
her consultation/case history was
mirrored in her feet. Working through a
full treatment the sensitive areas were the
sinuses and eyes on both feet, the neck,
throat and teeth on both feet, the spine
generally, the kidneys and adrenals both
feet, the lymphatics on both feet, uterus
both feet and the ovary on the left foot.
The sciatic on both feet was also tender.
The majority of the reflex points were
sore and tender but with few crystalline
deposits.

Client feedback

Mrs GH arrived looking tired. Her skin is
quite red where the psoriasis patches are.
It is very flaky and dry and quite hot to
the touch. She has trained herself not to
scratch over the years and has learned to
live with it. However, the unsightly
appearance causes some stress. Mrs GH
looked tired and stressed when she
arrived for this treatment. She was

looking forward to having some time to
herself and relaxing.

She was a little apprehensive to start, but
soon got used to my touch. She was
quite sensitive all over, registering pain
on most of the identified reflex points.
She did feel comfortable and warm
throughout the treatment.

She felt quite tired and sleepy at the end
of the session but said that she found the
treatment enjoyable. Mrs GH was given a
glass of water and allowed to relax for a
while before getting off the couch and
putting her shoes back on.

Homecare advice given

Mrs GH was given a sheet outlining
general homecare advice. I suggested
that she try to include some water in her
daily fluid intake and apply some
moisturiser to her feet before bed each
night. An appointment was made for
treatment in one week's time. Mrs GH
was also advised of potential
contra-action in the form of a healing
crisis – increased energy, increased bowel
and bladder movements, coughing and
sneezing, changes in sleep patterns,
increased emotions, an increase in the
symptoms currently felt. I advised her
that these would pass if experienced, and
not to panic. Drinking more water and
resting would help if any of these were
experienced.

Recommendations for self-treatment

I showed her the reflex points for the
sinus and adrenal glands on her hands
and gave her the details of how/when to
self-treat.

Self reflection

Mrs GH needed to be positioned slightly
higher on the couch and with more
support under her ankles. I found it
difficult to reach the areas that I needed

to work without lifting the foot up quite high. Her feet were quite dry so I used a cream medium, which meant that I slipped over the points at times. I need to investigate using different mediums over the course of these treatments to find the most suitable.

TREATMENT 2

READING OF THE FEET
Local contraindications: none
Skin texture/areas of hard skin: Dry heels, slight improvement from last week – trying to use cream daily
Colour: Pink on soles, normal on top of feet
Flexibility: Good
Temperature: Cool to touch
Swelling/puffiness: None
Odour: Slight odour today but wearing old shoes which smell slightly
Foot position: Normal
Nail condition: Slight thickening in little toenails
Skeletal structure/arches of the feet: Normal

Treatment plan:
A full reflexology treatment was performed. Sensitivity felt in sinus and eye reflexes still. The thyroid helper was sensitive this week, together with the solar plexus and kidneys/adrenals. However, the liver and small intestine on the right foot was also sensitive this week. The lymphatics in the groin and the chest area, both feet, also sensitive. The sciatic and reproductive organs were also sensitive as were points on the spine.

Client feedback
Mrs GH still appeared tired, but she has worked some extra shifts this week. Between treatments Mrs GH felt more relaxed and felt that she slept a little better. Her ears seemed a little congested and she expelled a lot of mucus the morning after the last treatment. Sinus congestion still a problem and she had a mild headache after the last treatment. This did pass quite quickly though. Psoriasis patches still widespread, red and flaky. Some tingling in her fingers this week but the weather has been cold, and she has not always remembered her gloves.

She quickly relaxed on the couch but was a little cold, so an extra blanket was provided. She did not fall asleep but relaxed with her eyes closed for most of the treatment. However, her facial expressions denoted that most of the reflex points found were still very painful. She felt thirsty afterwards and needed to go to the toilet. When she returned from the toilet she sat down and drank some water, whilst we went through the homecare advice.

Homecare advice given
She has been trying to drink more water, but has not been very successful. She has been applying cream to her feet each night, and the fissures are much softer this week, although they will take a long time to heal. Appointment made for one week's time.

Recommendations for self treatment
I reminded Mrs GH of the hand reflexology points, and this week included the hip and back. Working the hands will also improve the circulation in them.

Self reflection
I applied less cream and more pressure this week. As a result I did not slip off points as much. I got quite hot during the treatment and had to drink plenty after the client left – I must try to stay hydrated myself this week.

TREATMENT 3

READING OF THE FEET

Local contraindications: none

Skin texture/areas of hard skin: Dry, heels show improvement from last week – now using aqueous cream daily

Colour: pale pink but toes slightly blue

Flexibility: Good

Temperature: Cool to touch

Swelling/puffiness: None

Odour: No discernable odour

Foot position: Normal

Nail condition: Slight thickening in little toenails

Skeletal structure/arches of the feet: Normal

Details of how the therapist conducted the treatment

A full reflexology treatment was performed. Sensitivity was felt this week in the same areas as last treatment although there has been some movement. Some points appear to be shifting and getting less sensitive. The sinus and lymphatics are still apparent, as were the kidneys and adrenals. The thyroid helper is still also sensitive. The sciatic nerve this week seems fine on the right foot – so some progress is being made.

Client feedback

Mrs GH reported that she had felt much more relaxed and felt that she slept much better. She has found it easier to get to sleep this week - 'I can shut my brain off quicker'. Sinus congestion has eased a little. Psoriasis patches are not as angry and red as they were and many appear to be healing. Mrs GH felt fine at the start of the treatment. She appeared more alert but still relaxed and calm.

She was quite talkative at the start of the treatment asking and answering questions. She did relax as the treatment progressed and became quieter. Her toes were slightly blue at the start of the treatment but as I worked they regained their normal colour. She said that her hands and feet have felt cold this week but cannot explain why.

She felt relaxed but not tired. She said that she was pleased with the way things are progressing and feels that reflexology is having a positive effect on her. She had a glass of water and got off the couch slowly.

Homecare advice given

Mrs GH has managed to drink more water this week, so we discussed the possibility of cutting down on her caffeine intake. She feels that she needs to drink caffeine to keep her going during a busy and stressful shift. I suggested possible alternatives such as Rooibos tea, decaffeinated tea and coffee and herbal teas. She did not seem too impressed by these suggestions however but said that she might give the decaffeinated coffee a try.

Recommendations for self treatment

She is continuing to try and work on her own reflex points on her hands, but keeps forgetting! I suggested that she do them in the evening if she is watching television, rather than trying to fit them in between patients and tasks at work which is what she has been trying to do.

Self reflection

I feel more confident when working on Mrs GH now – I feel that I am getting to know her feet and the type of treatment that she requires. I can apply a good firm pressure, in fact, I need to. She may be less sensitive in some areas, as she is standing all day at work. I think that this makes people less aware of what they are actually feeling, as they learn to override sensations of pain in the feet and legs. She also seems pleased that although the same areas are sensitive, there seem to be fewer points and a decrease in pain /sensitivity levels. Her overall levels of wellbeing are showing an improvement – she is sleeping well and is more relaxed. Her psoriasis is now showing definite signs of improvement.

TREATMENT 4

READING OF THE FEET
Local contraindications: none
Skin texture/areas of hard skin: Much better – skin well moisturized and fissures are beginning to heal and close up
Colour: Pink on soles, normal colour on top
Flexibility: Good
Temperature: Cool to touch
Swelling/puffiness: None
Odour: Slight odour today but wearing old shoes again, which smell slightly
Foot position: Normal
Nail condition: Slight thickening in little toenails
Skeletal structure/arches of the feet: Normal

Details of how the therapist conducted the treatment
A full reflexology treatment was performed. The sinus, neck, hip and sciatic reflex points were particularly sensitive today. The knees were also sensitive, and the spine, adrenals, kidney and liver on the right hand side.

Client feedback
Mrs GH seemed less tired today. She thinks her energy levels are improving. She relaxed into the treatment quickly and almost fell asleep. Her nose was running after the last treatment – and did so for the next day or so. She has not experienced any tingling in her fingers showing an improvement in her circulation and her hands and feet felt warmer this week. She had to reschedule the planned appointment and felt that she missed the treatment – almost as if her system was expecting it! She has latterly experienced sinus pain and an increase in congestion in her head. She had to take sinus tablets for this at the weekend as the pain became too intense. She had a perm on her hair three days ago and has been rubbing down her bathroom cabinets. As a result, she has been exposed to excessive dust and chemicals since her last treatment which might explain the sinus problems. She did not wear a mask for the DIY which I recommended for use in the future.

Continuing Professional Development requirements
Having seen improvements in the general health of Mrs GH, a client who is on her feet for many hours each day, I would like to explore the subject of Vertical Reflexology and its applications in the workplace. As a result of this case study, I have requested course information and dates with a view to extending my knowledge and gaining more experience using reflexology in a care setting.

How the client felt during the treatment
The sinus areas were very sensitive today. The sciatic and hip reflexes are now evident again – perhaps due to the bout of DIY? She felt relaxed throughout the treatment.
Mrs GH was quite thirsty afterwards. She had two glasses of water immediately after treatment and took her time getting off the couch today.

Homecare advice given

Mrs GH is now drinking more water albeit in the form of diluted lemon barley water – but at least this is an improvement on coffee. She should continue to apply cream to her feet on a daily basis and come for reflexology regularly.

Recommendations for self treatment

She has tried some hand reflexology but is finding it difficult to fit it into her daily routine. Mrs GH needs to get her wheat allergy checked professionally and avoid overexposure to chemical and dust, as these clearly aggravate her sinus problems.

Self reflection

Her sinus reflexes this week were particularly painful. I applied the usual pressure that I work with but she found it too uncomfortable. I had to reduce the pressure considerably in these areas to stay within her tolerance levels. This surprised me, as Mrs GH normally likes a reasonable amount of pressure and is able to withstand it. Last treatment I was able to apply a good, firm pressure throughout the treatment. This reflects a direct correlation between client lifestyle and findings on the feet. Mrs GH's DIY and hair treatments appear to have made her sinus congestion worse. Her feet certainly seemed to show this. Her skin, however, continues to show signs of improvement although the chemical and dust ingestion could become apparent in her skin at a later date – the psoriasis could 'flare' up within a few days. I must note this on the next consultation and continue to monitor it.

TREATMENT EVALUATION

Mrs GH's expectations of treatment were:

- To calm and heal her psoriasis
- To improve her sleeping patterns and help her relaxation
- To help stress levels
- To ease sinus congestion

Throughout the course of four treatments, Mrs GH has seen as improvement in all of the areas that she required. Her ability to relax has increased and she is now sleeping more deeply, and for longer. As a result, her stress levels have dropped as she does not feel as fatigued during the day. She is able to 'switch her brain off' at the end of the day. Her psoriasis is improving – it often gets worse during times of stress, so this is a welcome effect of the reflexology treatments. Her sinus congestion has also improved, but this system is easily irritated as demonstrated during the last week of treatment. She has managed to drink more fluid which may also be helping ease sinus congestion.

All of her problems are chronic, and as a result may take many months to improve dramatically. However, with the simple changes that have been made by the client and the regular reflexology treatments, improvements have been felt. This has also been noted by changes in the foot charts – with reflex points disappearing completely or less sensitivity being felt in certain points. A client with many health issues can seem daunting to an inexperienced therapist, but chronic conditions present great challenges. Both the client and therapist need to persevere, as changes in health and wellbeing may be slow to effect. Mrs GH is keen to continue with reflexology alongside orthodox medical practices. She will now have a break as her GP starts a course of medicine and will recommence reflexology once her medicine levels have been ascertained. Mrs GH thoroughly enjoyed her reflexology treatments and felt that she benefited from time spent relaxing. She will try to work on her own hands to continue the benefits and will continue to use reflexology in the future.

Continuing Professional Development requirements
Having seen improvements in the general health of Mrs GH, a client who is on her feet for many hours each day, I would like to explore the subject of Vertical Reflexology and its applications in the workplace. As a result of this case study, I have requested course information and dates with a view to extending my knowledge and gaining more experience using reflexology in a care setting.

You know now what a detailed case study looks like and how treatments should be recorded and reflected upon.

9 The holistic approach

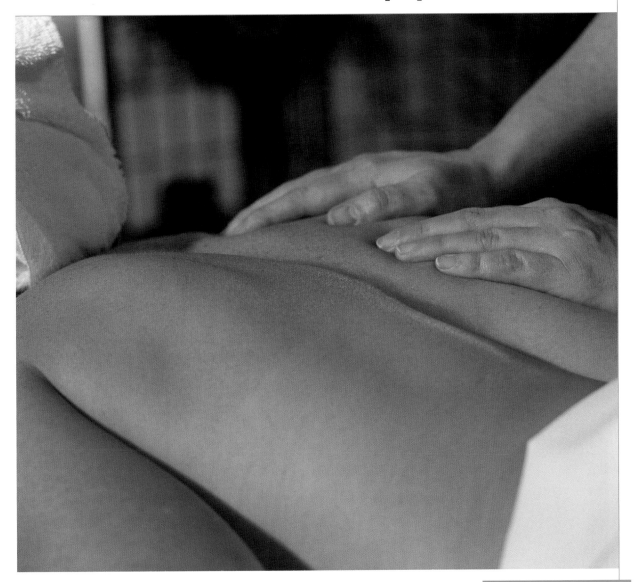

In Brief

The first section of this chapter explains the holistic approach, integral biology and why they are important for practising reflexologists; the second describes stress and its effect and the third explains how a holistic approach and reflexology can help in the treatment of hospital and hospice patients.

Learning objectives

The target knowledge of this chapter is:
● the holistic approach
● integral biology
● stress
● the use of reflexology in a care setting.

THE HOLISTIC APPROACH

THE HOLISTIC APPROACH & INTEGRAL BIOLOGY

What is the holistic approach?

The term holistic comes from the Greek word holos meaning whole. The holistic approach or treatment takes into account a person's whole being, not just the physical symptoms or problems but also psychology, environment and nutrition and the effects, both positive and negative, that these can have on the body as a whole.

What is integral biology?

Integral biology is the study of our environment's effect on our physical and mental health. Everything we do in our daily lives affects our bodies. For example, an uncomfortable working environment can cause stress, tiredness and related conditions such as anxiety, depression and heart conditions. At home lack of exercise and a poor diet plus too much sedentary activity (watching TV, writing, reading, using computers) may cause similar problems.

Sitting correctly whilst using a computer can prevent physical problems/damage such as carpal tunnel syndrome and backache.

What affects integral biology?

There are many factors that influence our integral biology. Some are negative and some positive.

Negative factors
- lack of exercise
- processed food
- chemically-treated fruit and vegetables
- lack of fresh air
- too much alcohol
- a stressful job
- bereavement or grief
- too much caffeine (tea, coffee, cola)
- lack of sleep
- financial problems
- worries about family/relationships
- too much time spent on or near electro-magnetic equipment (computers, photocopiers)
- a smoky or poorly ventilated home or office
- internalising problems and worries.

Positive factors
- regular exercise
- eating fresh fruit and vegetables
- a varied and healthy diet
- drinking lots of water
- taking regular breaks at work and home
- reorganising work patterns to avoid sitting or standing in the same place for several hours in a row
- getting enough sleep
- getting plenty of fresh air and making sure a window is open when someone is smoking.

How can these problems be treated by reflexology?

Imbalances in the external environment can cause imbalances internally. It is therefore important to take any apparently external factors into account before trying to treat physical symptoms. Poor circulation might appear to be a serious blood problem, but may be caused by lack of exercise and a diet lacking in nutrients. Reflexology treats the symptom (e.g. headaches) as well as the real cause (e.g. stress, insomnia) thus rebalancing the body both physically and psychologically. Combined with necessary changes in lifestyle and diet it can be as effective, or more so, than traditional medicine which treats a specific problem, not the whole body.

How can a reflexologist find out what is the real cause?

By careful questioning and discussion. When a client attends a treatment the reflexologist needs to find out as much as possible about the person and the problem (see Consultation Techniques in Chapter 7). Topics covered should include medical history, contraindications to treatment, current illnesses or physical/psychological conditions, family details, type of work and working conditions, stress at work and at home, hobbies, lifestyle (i.e. sedentary, active, relaxed, stressed), diet and exercise. The reflexologist should also look for non-verbal clues such as nervous habits and poor posture that provide information on the client's day-to-day life. On subsequent visits the reflexologist should check for any changes and discuss these with the client.

Can reflexology alone cure the real cause once it is discovered?

In some cases, yes. However, the reflexologist may offer aftercare advice, explaining how reflexology is part of the process of healing and not a miracle cure and that if the conditions that caused the problem in the first place continue then the problem will continue as well. Also, it is important to remember that reflexology is complementary to traditional, or allopathic, medicine rather than a replacement for it. Where appropriate it can be used at the same time as traditional medicine.

Why is a holistic approach important?

Because it treats each person individually and in the context of their own life. This enables people to improve their health themselves thus re-establishing the body's equilibrium, known as homeostasis. Furthermore, for the best therapeutic effect, all aspects of integral biology need to be considered.

You now know about the holistic approach and integral biology. The next section explains stress and how reflexology can be used to combat it.

In order to live a healthy life you must eat fruit and vegetables, sleep well and exercise regularly.

THE HOLISTIC APPROACH

THE CAUSES OF STRESS AND ITS EFFECTS

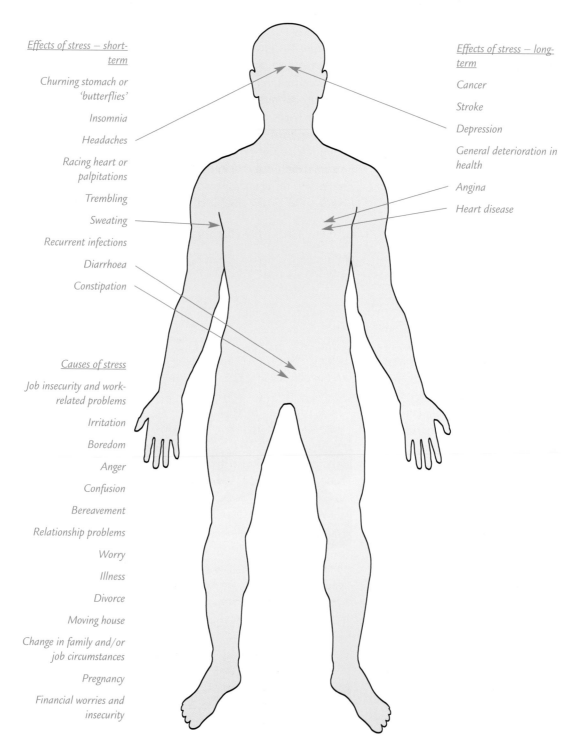

Effects of stress – short-term

Churning stomach or 'butterflies'

Insomnia

Headaches

Racing heart or palpitations

Trembling

Sweating

Recurrent infections

Diarrhoea

Constipation

Causes of stress

Job insecurity and work-related problems

Irritation

Boredom

Anger

Confusion

Bereavement

Relationship problems

Worry

Illness

Divorce

Moving house

Change in family and/or job circumstances

Pregnancy

Financial worries and insecurity

Effects of stress – long-term

Cancer

Stroke

Depression

General deterioration in health

Angina

Heart disease

Causes of stress and its effects.

What is stress?

Stress is any factor that threatens our physical or mental well-being. Such factors can be imagined (worry about the future) or real (financial problems). It is not the factor itself that is damaging but the response to it. Some people have very stressful lives but manage stress so that it does not affect them whereas for others even the slightest worry can have damaging consequences.

How does stress affect us?

The body has always had to respond to stress. Thousands of years ago, stress factors were more physical: humans needed to hunt for their food, protect themselves from wild animals and secure shelter. In the twenty-first century stress factors are likely to be more intangible: job insecurity, worrying about relationship difficulties, irritation about traffic jams. However, the effects of stress are exactly the same whether the threat is an angry boss or an angry buffalo! The body, perceiving danger, prepares to face it or run away (the fight or flight syndrome). Several systems shut down and the body works to conserve energy to enable movement and escape: adrenaline rushes into the body to warn of impending danger and the heart rate increases, the blood vessels contract increasing blood pressure, the digestive functions shut down and the muscles contract.

If the perceived danger is then removed or escapes, the stress response has achieved its aim and the body relaxes. However, usually, it is not easy to get away from the cause of the stress. Most stress factors are no longer responded to with activity: it is very hard for an office worker to run away from an annoying problem or colleague. As a result the body remains tense and cannot relax. It is this unused response mechanism which is damaging.

How is stress damaging?

It has been estimated that stress is the cause of 75% of disease. In the short term, as a response to perceived danger, stress is literally life-saving. If we didn't feel stress we would not make the effort to cross the road a little faster to get out of the way of an approaching car, or perform at a heightened rate in a sports match or competition in order to win. However, in the long term, if a person continues to feel stress in response to external factors but does nothing either to remove the cause of the stress or to respond to it differently, the stress reaction can be damaging. The body remains in a state of alert and eventually this will have a physical effect on the systems concerned.

What are the symptoms of stress?

Anyone who has ever been nervous about an interview, exam, meeting or important football match has felt some of the symptoms of stress.

These include: churning stomach or 'butterflies', racing heart or palpitations, diarrhoea, loss of appetite, trembling, insomnia, sweating. In the medium term these symptoms, left untreated, may cause chest pains, allergies, persistent insomnia, high blood pressure, abdominal pain, migraines, depression, ulcers, asthma and infections. In the long term constant stress is known to cause heart disease, strokes, cancer, angina and may be fatal.

How can stress be cured?

Stress in itself cannot be 'cured' because threats to our well-being will always exist around us. However, it is not the threat but the way it is perceived and responded to that is most important. If stress is managed it is no longer damaging, e.g. if stuck in traffic, one driver may become enraged whereas

THE HOLISTIC APPROACH

another will accept that this is a normal situation in a busy area. The first driver is responding to stress, the second is managing it. However, the actual stress factor itself is the same.

How can stress be managed?
By learning to respond in a healthier way and using relaxation techniques. We cannot simply tell our bodies to relax; we have to learn how to relax them, via particular relaxing activities as well as with specific breathing, visualisation and relaxation techniques.

How can reflexology help
When the body is stressed it must work harder than usual in order to remain balanced. Hence, stressed people tend to over-use conventional relaxation methods such as drinking and smoking in order to reach the same calm as the less stressed. Reflexology brings the body back into balance, restoring homeostasis and inducing deep relaxation which helps to remove the pent-up tension of the stress response. It boosts the immune system, which is weakened by constant stress, stimulates the circulation, removes toxins, stabilises breathing, boosts energy levels and induces calm in both mind and body. As a one-off it can help the body to recover from stress; as a continuous treatment or series of treatments it can help the client to learn how to relax and therefore how to manage the stress that caused the problem in the first place.

You now know what stress is and how reflexology can be used to combat it. The final section in this chapter explains how reflexology may be used in a care setting such as a hospital or hospice.

THE USE OF REFLEXOLOGY IN A CARE SETTING

When is reflexology suitable in hospital?
A general and gentle overall treatment is useful in most cases, on the hands where the feet cannot be touched. Patients who cannot move around a lot often suffer from poor blood and lymphatic circulation and reflexology is very helpful in stimulating these. The therapist should take into account any prescribed medication and possible contraindications. Where possible privacy should be maintained, even if it is simply drawing the curtain around a bed. In these circumstances, consent forms may be signed by the client or their primary carer prior to the treatment.

When is it not suitable?
The therapist needs to know of any contraindications to treatment and prescription medicines the patient is taking. The reflexologist can ask the doctor to sign a letter of consent specifying the type of treatment to be performed. Some healthcare trusts decline written permission due to an increase in litigation but many doctors feel that their patients are able to take decisions about their own health.

What precautions need to be taken in this environment?
Therapists who are able to work in a care setting should be aware of and comply with any existing care plans and should keep detailed consultation forms and records. They should always work with the approval of client and primary carer.

Is it available on the NHS?
Reflexology is not, at the time of writing, fully available through NHS doctors and

hospitals, but many practices and private hospitals offer it as a service which patients may pay for if they wish. There are, however, several pioneering hospitals which offer reflexology to both patients and staff.

Is reflexology suitable for people with disabilities or special needs?

Many who suffer from disabilities and special needs experience muscle spasm, problems with digestion and excretion, lowered immunity and insomnia. Some suffer physical conditions caused by their repetitive or limited movements. Reflexology can help with all of these problems, helping to relax the body, boost immunity, improve sleep patterns, balance digestion and excretion and reduce spasms. It is also a contact therapy which can boost the self-esteem of the client. The therapist should check with the disabled client and his/her primary carer and GP to ensure that there are no contraindications to treatment.

Can reflexology be used with the elderly?

For many elderly people the stress of bereavement, the loss of their home, moving to a new area and making new friends, is often coupled with ill-health. Loss of physical contact also plays a large part as people age, lose their partners and friends and become withdrawn as a result of change. Various conditions that affect the elderly, particularly lowered immunity, respiratory problems, depression, insomnia, digestive congestion and urinary problems, can be helped by reflexology because it helps to boost the immune system, induce relaxation and calm, help balance sleep patterns and regulate digestive and urinary systems.

It is also a way for an elderly person to feel the healing qualities of touch

without the invasion of privacy that other therapies, such as massage, might involve. With every elderly client, it is especially important to make a detailed individual assessment of their needs, expectations and their current state of health. The client's joints may be stiffer, their skin weaker and frailer and their circulation not as efficient as a younger person's. These factors should be taken into account when reading and treating the feet and a gentler or possibly shorter treatment administered if necessary.

Chiropractor with patient.

Can reflexology help the terminally ill?

Reflexology is known to induce calm and deep relaxation and is thus very helpful for the terminally ill and their families. The combination of touch and stress relief can help soothe pain and reduce anxiety. As with any treatment, the reflexologist must check that there are no contraindications and obtain consent from the client's GP.

Are there any reflexes that are particularly helpful in this setting?

Patients finding themselves in a hospital, nursing/residential home, hospice, or rehabilitation unit are often stressed as a result of changes in their health and home environment. This may show physically or mentally; anxiety, depression, frustration and anger are common as are muscle and joint pains, headaches, digestive disorders, oedema and circulatory problems. A general overall treatment is usually the most useful with a focus on a specific reflex or body system when required. For those whose feet cannot be treated a hand reflexology treatment is just as effective and, in cases where human contact and touch has been lacking, it can be more so not only because the therapist is closer to the client but also because holding another person's hand is a sign of intimacy and warmth.

You now know about the holistic approach and integral biology, stress and how reflexology can be used to combat it and how reflexology may be used in a care setting such as a hospital or hospice.

10 Other complementary therapies

In Brief
Reflexology is only one of many complementary and holistic therapies. This chapter gives a brief overview of others.

Learning objectives ●

The target knowledge of this chapter is:
● the definition of other complementary therapies.

OTHER COMPLEMENTARY THERAPIES

Acupuncture

An ancient Chinese therapy, now being used more and more in the West, acupuncture is the insertion of very fine needles into the skin at certain points to help relieve pain and improve the body's own healing mechanisms. The points are on meridians (energy channels). If there is a blockage in energy then a part of the body connected to that meridian may become ill or weak. The needles are thought to release the blockage and help the body to heal itself.

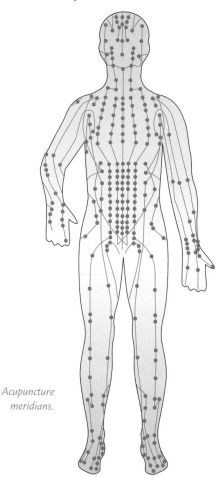

Acupuncture meridians.

Acupressure

A manual pressure technique using the hands, elbows, arms, knees and feet to stimulate and rebalance body energy. Woking in the same way as Shiatsu, acupressure clears blockages in key body points allowing energy to flow freely along the meridians.

Alexander technique

The Alexander technique encourages healing and better health through better posture and awareness of how the body is used. It is especially useful for backache and headaches. It was developed by an actor called Frederick Mathias Alexander who discovered that improving his posture stopped him losing his voice.

Aromatherapy

Aromatherapy is the use of essential plant and flower oils for their therapeutic properties, either in massage, inhalations, or vaporisers. Treatment can be used for medical or non-medical purposes, for relaxation or healing.

Ayurvedic medicine

Ayurveda means knowledge (ayur) of life (veda). Body harmony and good health are achieved through proper diet, exercise, lifestyle and meditation, specific to a client's constitution or mix of doshas, or body elements – vata, pitta and kapha. It focuses on rebalance or attunement to the correct dosha rather than the exclusive treatment of symptoms. Widely practised in India, it is a philosophy and a lifestyle as well as a medicine.

Bach flower remedies

Dr Edward Bach, a doctor and a practising homeopath, turned away from both traditional medicine and homeopathy believing that there was a more natural and holistic way to treat illness. He developed 38 remedies, which are infusions of plants with water and alcohol, based on his research in the countryside. The remedies aim to treat mental and emotional problems, which often precede and cause physical symptoms.

Bodywork

There are various forms of bodywork, many with cultural foundations such as Shiatsu, Lomi Lomi, Kahuna massage, Amma massage, Marma Point massage, Heller work, Rolfing and holistic massage. While these types focus on treatment of the body through manipulation of the soft tissues others, such as chiropractic and osteopathy, focus on manipulation of the joints.

Bowen technique

The Bowen technique, developed in Australia by Thomas A. Bowen, aims to rebalance the body holistically using gentle moves on tissues. A Bowen practitioner can feel whether muscles are stressed or tense and use the moves to release this build-up. The light rolling movements stimulate the body's energy flows. It is not a massage or a manipulation but a gentle process that encourages the body to heal itself.

Colour therapy

Colour therapy is the therapeutic use of colour and light applied to specific points (acupoints) to rebalance body energy. Performed using coloured fabrics, candles, liquids, and gemstones often in the shape of wands or prisms. Also used as part of Ayurvedic medicine; the seven main chakras have specific colours associated with them.

Chiropractic

A chiropractor manipulates the joints of the body, specifically the spine, in order to relieve pain. It works on the basis that

Some herbs used in Chinese medicine.

pain is often caused by a nerve which is not functioning properly and thus the spine, which the central nervous system runs through, is the focus of the therapy. It is especially useful for any lower back and neck pains as well as headaches.

Crystal Therapy

A vibrational therapy involving placement of specific crystals on the chakras to rebalance the body energies and improve health. Crystals such as rose quartz and amethyst are used during treatments.

Ear Candling

Also known as thermo-auricular therapy, ear candling involves placing a specialised candle in the ear canal and lighting the opposite end. This is thought to create a low-level vacuum that draws out earwax and impurities, relieving pressure in the head and sinuses.

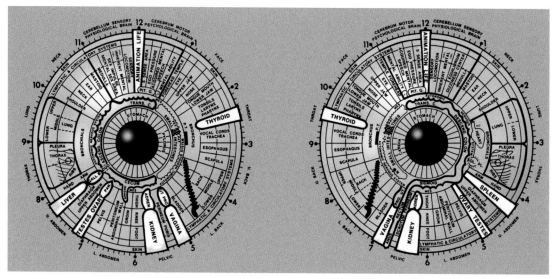

Iridology charts.

Herbalism

Herbalism is the use of plants, usually the whole plant, to make herbal remedies. It is an ancient, traditional medicine — what is now considered traditional medicine only replaced it in the last three hundred years.

Holistic massage

These techniques use classical Swedish massage techniques to treat physical and psychological problems. Routines usually cover the body and can include movements performed on the face and scalp. Pressure varies depending on the area of the body being worked upon and client requirements.

Homeopathy

Homeopathy treats like with like. By using minute doses of the bacteria, virus or substance which has caused the problem in the first place (i.e. cat hair in a remedy for an allergy to cat hairs), the treatment builds up the patient's resistance and immunity to the problem substance or bacteria. Many homeopathic remedies have to be used and even stored well away from strong smells because such smells can reduce their effectiveness.

Hypnotherapy

A treatment where the therapist induces a deep state of relaxation in the client by using a soothing, monotonous tone of voice. Thought to bring about a different level of consciousness where the client becomes receptive to suggestion. Commonly used to assist with changing habits such as smoking or overeating and states such as anxiety.

Indian Head Massage

A traditional form of head massage, using specific techniques covering only the head, neck and upper back. This treatment is very effective in treating stress, headaches and eyestrain.

Iridology

By studying the irises (the coloured parts of the eyes) of a patient and noting any changes, iridologists can diagnose physical and psychological problems.

Kinesiology

Kinesiology is a holistic treatment that focuses on testing the muscles and energy meridians to discover and then treat the body's imbalances on all levels: chemically, energetically, physically and mentally. Using different positions and the application of pressure to the limbs, the kinesiologist can determine whether there are any energy blocks in the body and correct them through firm massage. Kinesiology is preventative and, like many complementary therapies, aims to treat the whole person.

Lymphatic drainage massage

A gentle form of massage that uses superficial movements on the skin to move lymphatic fluid towards lymph ducts, the heart and ultimately into the systemic circulation. The lymphatic system plays an important role in the immune system. It is used to treat lymphodema, swelling in the limbs caused by lymph accumulation.

Naturopathy

Naturopathy is a therapy that combines 'natural' healing practices such as herbal remedies, hydrotherapy and diet with modern methods of testing, such as x-rays to ascertain problems and rebalance health.

Neurolinguistic Programming

Developed in the 1970s by Richard Bandler and John Grinder, NLP focuses on changing pattens of metal and emotional behaviour through self-awareness and effective communication. Thought to be useful for the treatment of nervous system disorders such as phobia and depression.

Osteopathy

Like a chiropractor, an osteopath manipulates the joints of the body. Osteopaths work on the basis that the body's structure and function are interdependent: if the structure is damaged in any way it will affect the function. By manipulating joints and bones they can correct structural problems which will improve the body's function.

Physiotherapy.

Physiotherapy

Physiotherapy uses physical exercises, massage and the application of pressure to relieve physical pain and muscular tension. It is often used to re-educate the body in cases of major surgery, illness, or an accident.

Reiki/spiritual healing

Reiki means universal life force energy in Japanese and Reiki healers act as channels for this universal energy to pass into the patient/client. By using hands in certain positions on different parts of the body, the healer is said to draw energy to the body, promoting healing, balance and relaxation.

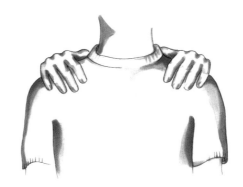

Reiki.

Shiatsu

Shiatsu is a form of acupressure: the use of finger or thumb pressure on points along meridians (energy channels) to

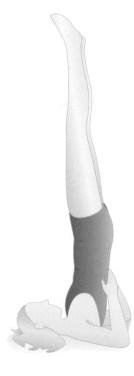

*Yoga posture –
a shoulder stand.*

help relieve pain and encourage the body to heal itself. The pressure points are the same as those used in acupuncture.

Stone Therapy

The use of heated and cooled stones applied through massage or indirect application to the body to relax and rejuvenate muscles and circulation. Different temperatures stimulate the body's natural healing responses to balance mind, body and spirit. Also known as geothermal therapy.

Swedish Massage

Modern massage is based on techniques developed by Per Henrik Ling. He developed a system of movements which he found helpful for improving health. The system he developed, based on Chinese techniques, form the classical massage techniques used today. Originally performed using talcum powder, and incorporating many vigorous movements, Swedish massage is often today performed with oil.

Subtle energy/vibrational medicine

A form of therapy that views the body as an 'energy system'. It uses natural resonance to restore the flow of body energy; therapies such as acupuncture, aromatherapy, Bach flower therapy, chakra rebalancing, channeling, colour therapy, crystal healing, absent healing, flower essence therapy, homeopathy, reiki or polarity therapy harness subtle energy frequencies and channel them to induce healing.

Therapeutic touch

A therapy that involves gentle 'laying-on' of hands to invoke a healing response. The therapist uses their hands to detect imbalances in the body.

Traditional Chinese Medicine

TCM is an ancient system of health care from China that is based on a concept of balanced qi or vital energy, which is believed to flow throughout the body. The opposing forces of yin (negative energy) and yang (positive energy) influence qi, and these forces are thought to regulate the balance of mind, body and spirit. A disruption in qi brings about disease. TCM practitioners use herbal and nutritional therapy, exercise, meditation, acupuncture, and massage to restore balance and health.

Vertical Reflexology

This therapy focuses on the weight bearing dorsal reflexes rather than the soles of the feet. Treatments are performed with the client standing to access deep reflexes. The feet are thought to be more sensitive as a result of weight bearing, and treatments are normally shorter in duration than classical reflexology.

Yoga/meditation

Both yoga and meditation have long been known to have beneficial, holistic effects and they are very useful self-help therapies. They teach the learner to have control of the body and mind. Yoga does this through physical exercise, including adopting different postures, relaxation techniques and breathing exercises. Meditation uses different focuses (such as visualisation, a candle, a mantra) to help a person find calm and a sense of their own centre. Meditation has the physiological effects of a short sleep, i.e. the body goes into the healing and recharging mode it adopts when we sleep, allowing the muscles to relax and the circulation to become more efficient.

You now know details about several other complementary therapies.

Bibliography

- Dwight C. Byers, *Better Health with Foot Reflexology: the Original Ingham Method* (Saint Petersburg, Florida: Ingham Publishing, 1990)

- Beryl Crane, *Reflexology: The Definitive Practitioner's Manual* (Shaftesbury: Element, 1997)

- Nicola M. Hall, *Reflexology: A Way to Better Health* (Bath: Gateway, 1991)

- Laura Norman with Thomas Cowan, *The Reflexology Handbook* (London: Piatkus, 1989)

- Vicki Pitman and Kay MacKenzie, *Reflexology: a Practical Approach* (Cheltenham: Stanley Thornes, 1997)

Acknowledgements

The publishers would like to thank the following for their invaluable assistance in the preparation of this book:

Rachael Kammerling – ITEC qualified Reflexologist
Rachel Moran – Model
Lorinda Taylor

Glossary

Acupoint: the pressure points along the energy meridians used in acupuncture or acupressure

Acupressure: ancient Chinese therapy using thumb or finger pressure at acupoints along energy meridians in the body to unblock energy

Acupuncture: ancient Chinese therapy using needles inserted at acupoints along energy meridians in the body to unblock energy

Ankhmahor: Egyptian physician whose tomb contains some of the earliest evidence of the use of foot massage

Anterior: front

Arch: instep of foot

Articulate: to join, particularly of bones

Bayly, Doreen: brought reflexology to Britain

Carpal: wrist bone; eight in each wrist (hamate, capitate, trapezoid, trapezium, scaphoid, lunate, triquetral and pisiform)

Chiropractic: manipulating the joints of the body, especially the spine, to relieve pain

Contraindication: a reason why treatment should not be used

Deep: far from the surface

Holistic: affecting the whole person

Homeostasis: balance and equilibrium of the body

Ingham, Eunice: the woman who discovered and developed reflexology

Lateral: side

Leverage: pressure provided by working hand to help the thumb/finger that is working

Meridian: a theoretical line of energy running through the body, used in acupuncture/pressure and considered to be similar to reflexology zones

Metacarpal: hand bones; form palm of hand; five in each hand

Metatarsal: foot bones; form main part of foot; five in each foot

Midline: central line of body used by medical profession to denote parts of body and location

Phalange: toe/finger bone; 14 in hand and foot (three in each finger and two in big toe/thumb)

Posterior: back

Referral area: the areas in the arm and hand which correspond to those of the leg and foot and are used when the foot and ankle cannot be treated

Reflex: relationship between point on foot/hand and another part of the body

Reflex areas: areas on feet/hands that correspond to other parts of the body

Superficial: near the surface

Support hand: the hand used to support the foot during treatment

Tarsals: ankle bone; seven in each ankle (medial, intermediate and lateral cuneiforms, cuboid, navicular, calcaneus and talus)

Transverse lines/zones: three lines across the feet, defining zones for treatment

Working hand: the hand working during treatment

Zone: an energy area in the body running from top to toe, front to back; developed by Dr William Fitzgerald, there are ten in the body; considered to be similar to acupuncture/pressure meridians.

Index

143

INDEX

Index